POTATOES

101 Recipes

POTATOES

101 Recipes

by
Cornelia Adam

h.f.ullmann

Table of Contents

Foreword

Potatoes first found their way to Europe more than 400 years ago, and were introduced to North America by European colonists. Since then they have won their way into our saucepans, bottles, and industrial products with unparalleled success. They have inspired painters and writers and encouraged engineers to come up with useful new inventions. But above all, the constant stream of new potato recipes has made countless people happy and satisfied their hunger. Old varieties and new breeds make sure that both lovers of the unusual and large industrial producers get exactly the kind of potatoes they like to suit their individual needs. Few other vegetables have so many different forms and flavors. Out in the field, the tubers are nondescript and colorless, but served up on a plate they become the multifaceted king of vegetables. Enjoy the taste of fried or baked potatoes, or have them mashed, garnished, or puréed. Whichever preparation method you choose, we hope you will have a lot of fun and enjoy eating them.

For the Love of Potatoes

Success is obvious, but the intention is never clear.
That is why people will always judge all human stories by success.
FRIEDRICH RÜCKERT, 19TH-CENTURY LINGUIST, WRITER, AND POET

The potato — a cultural asset

Gift of the gods and fruit of the devil, aphrodisiac and remedy, the food of princes and the poor, cult object and art object, multitalented means of survival, the potato—the powerful tuber of the Incan empire—has been all of these things during a career that has already lasted more than 10,000 years. Today potatoes are one of the world's four most important food plants, alongside maize, rice, and wheat. They also help to provide the ever-increasing world population with a healthy food source. The main producers are China, India, and Russia.

Vil du redde liv?

Papas Peruanorum, colored print from the Hortus Eystettensis (Basilius Besler, 1613)

The true gold of the Incas

Once upon a time the mighty earth mother Pachamama gave the potato to the Indians of the Andean Plateau in Peru as a gift in order to ensure their survival. There, at a height of 11,500 to 13,000 feet (3,500 to 4,000 meters), where no other edible fruits or vegetables can flourish, the Indians were already growing potatoes thousands of years ago. They used this precious crop for both food and medicine, and in order to store it they invented the freeze-dried potato, which can keep almost indefinitely. (Please note, all you readers who love to experiment: Do not try this with our potatoes! All the potatoes we have must not be allowed to get frosted.)

We can also see how important potatoes were for the Andean Indians from the fact that they worshiped the spirit of the potato as the god of nature *Axomama* with various performances and rituals.

Unfortunately, when the Spanish conquered South America, in their feverish lust for gold they failed to recognize that in the potato they had actually already discovered the true gold of the Incas. And that is neither an exaggeration nor meant metaphorically. After all, a single world potato harvest today is worth more than all the gold the conquerors of the Incas brought back to Europe. The potato came to Europe with seafarers, pirates, and buccaneers. We will probably never know for certain whether Drake or Raleigh was the first to bring back the potato to the English court. The precise date of the arrival of the new vegetable from South America is also lost in the mists of time. There is evidence from historical sources that potatoes were already being cultivated in Spain in the late 16th century.

The potato has had a somewhat checkered career in Europe and it took around 200 years to become firmly established in cooking pots and on plates all around the world. However, it has now revolutionized menus, especially in Europe and North America, more radically than any other food before or since.

Ornamental plant, fruit of the devil, food for the people

When the potato reached Europe, it was at first mainly for its exotic flowers that the plant was admired at the courts of kings and princes. It was planted in parks and ornamental gardens, so that people could enjoy the colorful splendor. Scientists tended this rarity from the New World in botanical gardens, and of course people knew from the reports of members of the Spanish expeditions that the potato was a tasty food item. But why was the potato then condemned as the fruit of the devil?

The answer is quite simple. There is not a single mention of the potato in the Bible and the myth of its creation does not exactly inspire confidence. The story told by the Church was that the devil spat on the ground and the potato grew from the spittle. For the potato it was certainly a problem that botanically speaking it belongs to the nightshade family, like the dangerous "witches herbs" such as mandrake, henbane, and deadly nightshade. Incidentally, other vegetables such as tomatoes, peppers, eggplant, and chiles also come from the same family, but they were not under discussion at that time.

The church warned people against potatoes, a number of doctors blamed eating potatoes for serious illnesses (from consumption to leprosy) and then some people really did become gravely ill and many even died. A crucial misunderstanding brought the potato into disrepute. The fruits that develop from the potato flowers are the seed capsules and—like all the parts of the potato plant that grow above ground—they contain the poison solanine. This poison can also be found in the green patches that develop on many potatoes when they have not been correctly stored.

People learned that potatoes are different from apples, raspberries, or blueberries. The edible part does not develop from the flower; you have to dig up the underground tuber. And then came the next false conclusion. In many parts of Europe potatoes were known as "earth apples." In Austria and parts of Bavaria they are still called "Erdäpfel" and in France they are "pommes de terre"—literally apples of the earth. However, you can pick an apple, wash it, and eat it straight away. Doing the same with a potato is really not a pleasant experience. It was only when potatoes were cooked that the spell was broken and the tasty tubers could begin their conquest.

The first potatoes in Germany were grown back in 1647 in the Frankish area of Pilgramsreuth, now part of the city of Rehau in Bavaria, by a peasant farmer called Hans Rogler. King Frederick II of Prussia's great promotion of potato-growing did not begin until 100 years later. Failed wheat harvests and serious famines played their part in the increasing acceptance of potatoes. The modest root crop soon became the typical food of the poor, and often it really was the only thing that kept people alive. Many people also survived on potatoes during the last two world wars, because they could be grown almost everywhere and high yields could be produced on very small pieces of land. There is no other food plant anywhere in the world that produces so much high quality nourishment in such a small space (potatoes contain virtually

Ceremonial vessel in the form of an outsize potato with a human face (Peru, Moche culture, 200 AD)

The US State of Idaho, known as the Potato State, hired the young Marilyn Monroe for a potato advertising campaign.

all the essential nutrients for life). What a blessing! And what a tragedy it was when this blessing was suddenly transformed into a curse! The great Irish famine of the mid-19th century cost well over a million Irish lives and forced around 1.6 million Irishmen to emigrate—mostly to the United States. (It was about this time that the Kennedy and Reagan families emigrated there.)

What had happened? At that time the impoverished peasant population of Ireland under English rule lived almost exclusively on potatoes and all went well until 1845, when the entire potato harvest failed in Ireland (as well as in large parts of Europe). It was catastrophic for the Irish. The famine lasted six years—the first three years were the worst. The cause was the disease *Phytophthora infestans*, commonly called potato blight, which is still feared today. However, although this disease still exists, since 1928 there has been a fungicide to counter it. Unlike the Colorado beetle, the spread and effects of which can be seen and controlled, potato blight is caused by the spores of a minute fungus which are carried by the wind. After that, only a few days pass before a healthy potato field is transformed into a stinking morass. Today we know all about this, but back then it was catastrophic for the Irish. The Irish potato famine wrote world history in a number of ways. It was the only time—so far—in their long history when the potato was not a lifesaver.

Multitalented transformation artist and global player

For many years the potato was considered to be an old-fashioned calorie bomb, a boring accompaniment to fill people up and a conventional element of good plain cooking. It takes time to get rid of this kind of negative image. The Americans were pretty smart back in the 50s and 60s when they used Marilyn Monroe as an advertising icon for potatoes, firstly because she was definitely not a conventional housewife, and secondly because her outfit, appropriately created from coarse potato sacks, still showed off her curvaceous figure. Since then countless stars, models, and celebrities have promoted the potato as a natural elixir for a happy life. Potatoes have become trendy as a health product for internal and external use. The substances they contain help towards a smooth, delicate skin, firm fingernails, good eyesight, and a strong heart. What is more, not only do they satisfy your hunger, you can also happily lose up to a pound a day. After all 3½ oz (100 g) potatoes only contain about 68 calories—no more than an apple—because a potato consists of about 75% water. The rest is a ball of energy and concentrated health!

Left: Symbolic handover of the potato (W. Guntermann, c. 1950). Right: 19th-century portrait of Sir Francis Drake.

So it is hardly surprising to find that there is even a famous quotation about potatoes from the works of the German poet Goethe: "Round in the morning, mashed at noon, sliced in the evening, so it should be—that's healthy!"

Potatoes can be served in an incredible variety of ways. French fries and chips are the kids' favorites. Potato dumplings, potato pancakes, and mashed or roast potatoes are the cornerstones of the menu. French croquettes, Swiss rösti, Italian gnocchi, Irish stew, Greek moussaka, oriental potato soup, and Asian potato salad all bring an international flair to the kitchen. You can get potato bread from the baker's and find your own creative ways of using potato flour in cakes and gâteaux. However, for purists, the unbeatable highlight is potatoes boiled with the skins on. And to finish with, a potato-based spirit such as vodka. No wonder that potatoes have long been the darlings of both cooks and gourmets! They can be found on plates everywhere from state receptions to students' lodgings and from vegetarian bistros to five-star restaurants.

In fact we are permanently surrounded by potatoes, often without realizing it. The potato is a brilliant transformation artist, making it a challenge for researchers, scientists, and others who like tinkering with things.

Jörg Immendorff is a self-confessed potato fan, as can be seen from his self-portrait of 1995.

There are few areas of life in which potatoes do not play a part: gummy bears, soup cubes, medicines, cosmetics, ready meals, newspapers, textiles, wallpaper paste, vaccines, antibiotics, biodegradable waste sacks, disposable plates and cups, yogurt pots, party cutlery, paper towels, tissues, drawing blocks, books, soap, powder, toothpaste, skin cream, packaging materials, building materials, plastic rawlplugs, golf tees, cleaning agents, laundry starch, bio-spirit … the list could go on indefinitely. So what is the secret of how potatoes get into everything? Their strength lies in their starch!

Finally, a tip for the cold season: potatoes boiled in their skins as hand-warmers! This was popular back in the 19th century. However, fine ladies often took fright and dropped the unusually hot potatoes with a shrill scream before managing to put the heat source into their muffs, so the idea went out of fashion, and all that remains is the well-known saying "to drop someone or something like a hot potato."

Declarations of love in painting, writing, and sculpture

Over thousands of years potatoes have not only been the inspiration for practitioners of the art of cooking and ambitious gastronomes to come up with ideas for new creations. Countless declarations of love are also to be found in the fine arts (sculpture, painting), literature, music (from opera to rap), not forgetting the work of film-makers, designers, installation artists…

The potato has been celebrated with pencil and paintbrush by great artists such as Vincent van Gogh, Jean-François Millet, Max Liebermann, Salvador Dalí, Käthe Kollwitz, Max Pechstein, Carl Spitzweg, Heinrich Zille, Wilhelm Busch, Jörg Immendorff, Sigmar Polke, Joseph Beuys—to name but a few.

Poets and writers like Johann Wolfgang von Goethe, Heinrich Heine, Matthias Claudius, Theodor Fontane, Joachim Ringelnatz, Berthold Brecht, Truman Capote, Pablo Neruda, Günter Grass, and many, many more have written in praise of the potato.

Christoph Willibald Gluck, Louis Armstrong, George and Ira Gershwin, Ike Turner, the Talking Heads, and Jan Delay all waxed lyrical about potatoes. Monuments to the potato can be found in many countries all around the world, from Germany and Poland all the way to Japan, and there are even a few potato museums

on the planet (in the US, Canada, and Germany). How about in space? Not yet—but the potato has been there. In 1995 it was the first food plant sent up by NASA with Columbia on a trip to the moon, in order to test whether it could flourish in conditions of weightlessness. It passed the test, so it seems that for potatoes there is no "mission impossible."

Barbara Kosber, the Munich Potato Museum

This picture by F. D.Vuillefroy, a pupil of Millet (19th cent.), is entitled *Peasants harvesting Potatoes*.

Traditional potato-farming in Germany – as described by a Bavarian farmer

Farmer Hagl comes from Aubing, once a small idyllic village outside Munich but now in the outskirts of the city. He can clearly remember how as a young boy he went round to the people of Aubing with a tractor to fill their cellars with potatoes. "In the fall we poured 5 to 10 hundredweight into each person's cellar," he remembers. At the time the most popular potato was Ackersegen. People liked the taste, it was easy to grow and dig up.

Back then there was fierce competition for customers. "You had to get in early, if you wanted to sell your potatoes," says Hagl. "Whoever got there first could empty his trailer. Up at about 5 o'clock, dig up and sort, and off we went with the trailers."

The prices paid for a hundredweight then sound almost incredible today. Even though it was a real nuisance getting all those tons of potatoes out of the field within three weeks, nobody would have thought of doing without potatoes. People had known since the Middle Ages that the land only remains healthy if you grow something different on it every year. Potatoes are ideal as part of the three-field system.

However, potatoes only became really interesting in the Munich area when a major potato processing company moved there – 150,000 metric tonnes of potatoes were processed in Munich in 1964. It was easier for the Hagls to deliver potatoes to the processing plant and it was a more secure business than knocking on every door in Aubing, even though it meant driving the tractor through the center of Munich.

Nowadays it is hard for anyone to imagine that just 50 years ago trailers full of potatoes driving through streets, where grand department stores and groups of admiring tourists now stand, were a normal part of the scene.

In the 1960s a new bulk buyer entered the market, a company that is still producing potato flour for baking and cooking. "We were saved the effort of cleaning and sorting," says Hagl. But the actual potato was quite tender. The starchy Calla was certainly ideal for the industry but it was not so easy to dig up. The potatoes themselves were quite delicate, if the farmer didn't take care they

ended up in the harvester along with the rest of the plant. With the variety Albatros everything was much simpler. "Although this potato doesn't contain so much starch, in other respects it is really rewarding to handle," says Hagl.

After 50 years, the Hagls are still supplying potatoes to the same company. However, the young woman who now farms the land has started growing other varieties for the farm shop and her own kitchen—Bamberger Hörnchen, Linda, Primura, Ditta, and because her name is Monika, also the variety Monika. Her father thinks growing so many varieties is a bit daft: "If you don't keep a careful eye on things, you completely lose track of what's growing where." However, you can clearly see how proud he is of his daughter and the way she loves to experiment—and it tastes good into the bargain.

Traditional and modern on a farm. The father plants the potatoes and the daughter sells them in the farm shop, along with other regional products.

Potato Portraits

Nature hates uniformity and loves diversity.
BERNARD WERBER, B.1961, FRENCH WRITER OF SCIENCE FICTION

Wealth through diversity

There are many varieties of potato. In every country and region there are varieties that grow particularly well there and are preferred by the inhabitants. Of course new breeds are also constantly being brought on to the market and competing with the older varieties. One positive effect of this development is that people are once again starting to show interest in more unusual old varieties. The time has passed when floury, predominantly waxy, and waxy were sufficient criteria for distinguishing the different types. Potatoes with lovely names like Annabelle, Pink Fir Apple, Blauer Schwede, and Bamberger Hörnchen are once again to be found in specialist stores and farmers' markets, making potato-lovers' hearts beat faster.

Bamberger Hörnchen
Nicola
Carola
Grenaille, France
Primura, Italy
Désirée, Germany
Hansa, Germany
Roseval, France
Granola
Französische Hörnchen
Sieglinde
Primura, Germany

Rosen-Désirée
Aula
Princess, Holland
Spunta, Zypern
Bintje, Holland
Quarta
Maja
Grata
Spunta, Germany
Sweet potato, Brazil

Potato portraits

Floury

Ackersegen
Ackersegen has pale yellow flesh and a buttery flavor and has been a standard crop since 1929. It is the floury counterpart of Sieglinde, which can look back on an equally long history. Ackersegen stores well and is very versatile, as it can be used for baking, boiling, and mashing.

Afra
Afra has a rough skin, a strong aroma, and deep yellow flesh. Its fine grain and strong flavor make it particularly good for mashing. Afra can be found in many supermarkets and farmers' markets.

Bintje

Bintje
Bintje comes from the Netherlands, as you might guess from its name. This medium-early variety produces relatively large tubers and is therefore popular for use in the production of fries and chips. Its yellow flesh is slightly paler than the skin.

Blauer Schwede
Blauer Schwede, which is oval to round in shape, is especially popular for use in salads and gratins. The sweetish, slightly nutty flavor adds a special touch to every potato dish and the blue-veined flesh gives it a unique color. Blauer Schwede is also known as Blue Congo, Idaho Blue, and Sharon's Blue. The blue pigment is said to protect the cardiovascular system. The coloring is also credited with an anti-inflammatory effect.

Predominantly waxy

Anaïs
This predominantly waxy potato with pale yellow flesh is particularly good for roasting and gratins. Its skin does not burst when steamed and it remains firm.

Désirée
Désirée originates from the Netherlands. It looks very attractive with its pink skin and yellow flesh. This medium-early potato has a fruity, juicy taste and is particularly good for boiling with the skin on.

La Bonnotte
La Bonnotte, the queen of French potatoes, has yellow flesh and skin and is round in shape. The original grows on the French Island of Noirmoutier, where seaweed is used as fertilizer. It has a very delicate, creamy flavor. It is particularly good for boiling—both peeled and with the skin on—and as a salad potato.

Laura
Laura is a relatively new variety, first registered in 1998. This oval to round potato with a red skin and deep yellow flesh is particularly good for baking.

Lady Christl
Lady Christl is distinguished by its very intense aroma. It is medium sized and quite long in shape.

Mayan Twilight
The distinctively patterned Mayan Twilight is a fairly new breed from Scotland. It has a red skin with yellow patches and a slight taste of marzipan, which is why it is sometimes called marzipan potato.

Waxy

Annabelle
This very early, long oval potato has yellow flesh and a delicate aroma. In the Palatinate region of Germany it is harvested from the end of June.

Désirée (above) and Laura

Bamberger Hörnchen
Bamberger Hörnchen is the oldest German potato variety. It was first mentioned in 1850 in the vicinity of Bamberg, hence the name Bamberger Hörnchen. These small potatoes are long and curved in shape and have pale yellow flesh and a nutty flavor. They are especially popular with gourmets in southern Germany. The Hörnla, as it is known in some parts, has similarities with the French potato La Ratte.

Heide-Sieglinde
Sieglinde has a yellow skin, yellow flesh and long oval tubers. It was already one of the most popular varieties back in the 1930s. Heide-Sieglinde is special to the Luneburg Heath area, but the Sieglinde variety can also be found in all other regions of Germany.

Heideniere

Heideniere is a medium-early German variety. This potato, registered in 1954 gets its name from its longish, slightly kidney-shaped form (*Niere* is the German word for kidney). It has a delicately spicy, fatty flavor, making it especially good for boiling and for potato salad.

Linda

Linda had almost died out in Germany, but was saved by an extensive campaign. Its deep yellow flesh is considered to be particularly aromatic; connoisseurs even say it is "outrageously good." The name Linda stands for the struggle against monopolies and the recollection of good old varieties.

Nicola

Nicola is one of the varieties currently available in most supermarkets. It is long and oval, with a smooth skin and pale yellow flesh. As with all potatoes, if possible you should go for organically-grown quality.

Rosalie

Rosalie is a new breed from organic cultivation. It has pink flesh and pink skin and is a long oval shape. Its slightly fatty flavor makes it particularly suitable for salads and gratins and also for boiling.

Pink Fir Apple

This variety originates from the UK (England and Scotland). It is a long oval shape and has pink skin and yellow flesh. Its firm flesh makes it very good for boiling skin-on and for potato salad.

Sieglinde (above) and Nicola

Right: Blue / purple potatoes like Vitelotte (top left) and potato-like exotics such as the kuwai (top right) not only add color to the plate but also different nuances of flavor.

Produits

Storing potatoes

Almost everything was different 50 years ago and this also applies to the storage of potatoes.

In Germany at that time, the majority of potatoes intended for eating were sold directly to the local population in the fall, loose or in sacks, to be kept in cellars. The potatoes to be used in the spring (e.g. seed potatoes) were stored in clamps on the farms. Storehouses for potatoes were few and far between. All of this was very time-consuming and often associated with big losses resulting from decay, premature germination, or frost damage.

Nowadays storage in cellars and clamps is rare. Typical customers buy their potatoes in small packs all year round, usually as and when they need them. In order for this to work, in the meantime a system has grown up, with well-qualified potato farmers, of large plants—mostly run by industry-wide organizations—for the storage, processing, and marketing of potatoes, and distribution centers belonging to the major retail chains. When buying potatoes in small quantities for immediate use, as with other fruit and vegetables the question of shelf-life and storage requirements is no longer paramount for the purchaser, even though their high water content of around 80% means that potatoes are a perishable, easily damaged commodity. For this reason, a few points should be borne in mind.

Potatoes only retain their quality if they are protected from

- light, especially direct sunlight,
- frost and high temperatures,
- moisture,
- potatoes already affected by decay,
- lack of air, and
- excessive changes of air.

Mixing varieties should be avoided.

Potato tubers are living organisms, which react very sensitively to environmental conditions. Factors of particular importance during storage are respiration, evaporation, and the start of germination. Under the influence of light certain alkaloids are produced, in particular solanine and chaconine. After being affected by light for a few days, a clearly visible green discoloration can be seen beneath the skin. Potatoes in this condition should not be eaten. Temperature has a crucial influence on the speed of the metabolic processes in the tuber. The optimum temperature should be 37–41°F (3 to 5 °C), because that is when the respiration rate is at its lowest.

The more the temperature varies above or below the optimum, the greater the loss of mass in the tuber due to respiration. At temperatures of around 34 °F (+1 °C) the potatoes become sweet; below freezing point they become frosted and are no longer fit for consumption. At temperatures above 46 °F (8 °C) potatoes slowly begin to germinate, if they have not previously been treated with germination inhibitors. The food value of potatoes that have germinated is considerably reduced.

Protection from moisture is also very important. A film of water around the tuber provides the best living conditions for certain putrefactive agents, which quickly ruin the potato. Just one decaying potato in a pack can infect those next to it and must therefore be removed immediately. In addition, potatoes must be stored in a way that allows them to respire unhindered.

If a potato has become dry as a result of excessive changes of air and the consequent increase in transpiration, it can be "refreshed" within an hour in a bain-marie (water bath).

It is also important to store packs of different varieties separately. Each variety has its own special properties. The consumer can tell these mainly from the different skin color, length of cooking time, and flavor.

In the big storage and packing businesses that predominate in the current market, potatoes are handled very carefully in accordance with the most recent state of research and the best experience in practice, and a great deal of technology is involved in controlling the climate in which they are stored, processed, and packed until the time comes to sell them. The use of cooling technology means that, when stored in this way, good quality can be maintained right through to July.

External defects on the tubers are usually harmless and will be removed during peeling. Internal defects, such as black discoloration of the flesh, are only permitted up to a certain limit. This also applies to damage caused by animals and other defects. However, most potatoes offered for sale look very attractive.

Nowadays far fewer potatoes are eaten in industrialized countries than in the past and they are eaten in a different ways. A high proportion are consumed in the form of processed products, such as chips.

Nevertheless, potatoes are still a genuine, very healthy food that can be prepared in a wide variety of different ways.

Prof. Dr. Peter Schuhmann, Rostock

Product Information

Every success has its secret, every failure its reasons.
JOACHIM KAISER, 20TH-CENTURY JOURNALIST, AUTHOR, AND CRITIC

It depends on the type

The success or failure of a potato dish depends very much on the type and variety of potato. Potato soups and mash only turn out well, if you use the right type. When buying it is essential to make sure you put the right kind in your shopping basket. Then (almost) nothing will stand in the way of your success.

On pages 26–28, we have described varieties of potatoes grown in Germany in the three texture categories of floury, predominantly waxy, and waxy. Similar varieties will be found in your area but most likely with different names—a little research will help you find the right match to use in your recipes.

Meersalz
Muskatnuss

Potatoes — a brief guide

There are hundreds of different varieties of potato, so you need to know what each one is best suited for and what to look out for when buying. If possible, look for organic potatoes, which can be bought in farmers' markets, organic stores, and increasingly often in supermarkets.

No matter which variety you decide on, the tubers should always be firm and unblemished. They should not have any damp or green patches or have started to sprout.

The basic distinction is between floury, predominantly waxy, and waxy varieties and within each of these categories there are early, medium early, and main crop varieties.

Waxy potatoes

These have the lowest starch content of all varieties, but in return they contain more water and protein. In addition, they are mostly long in shape. They are perfect for potato salads, so they are often described as salad potatoes, but they are also ideal for fries, rösti, and roasting.

Predominantly waxy potatoes

These are the all-rounders of the species and can be used for every purpose. Their consistency is somewhere between waxy and floury. As they bind well with sauces, they make an ideal side-dish. Because of their higher starch content of 15%, they turn light brown when baked, roasted, or fried, while nevertheless remaining nice and light.

Floury potatoes

These varieties are distinguished by their floury consistency and quickly disintegrate during cooking because of their high starch content of 16.5%. They are excellent for making soups, mash, dumplings, gnocchi, potato noodles, and stews.

What else is out there

Heathland potatoes

Heathland potatoes originate from Luneburg Heath. This part of northern Germany is one of the oldest potato-growing areas in the country and has the best soil for growing varieties like Bintje, Heide-Sieglinde, Linda etc.

Marshland potatoes

Potatoes grown in marshy ground have a shiny, slightly greasy skin. The best-known of these is Moor-Sieglinde, which loves the slightly acid soil of marshes. When harvested, this potato comes out of the marshy ground looking as if it had already been washed.

Island potatoes

Island potatoes grow in sandy soil and are fertilized with eel grass. The main producers are the Île de Batz in Brittany and the island of Cyprus.

Mountain potatoes

Mountain potatoes are grown at a height of 1,970–3,280 feet (600 to 1,000 meters). In Europe they are grown in places like Switzerland and the Forest Quarter of Austria. These potatoes grow relatively slowly in the rough ground, which gives them a more intense flavor.

The diversity of potatoes

Potatoes are with me all year round. At home we eat potato dishes several times a week. Potatoes never get boring, because they can be prepared in so many different ways. However, as I'm a potato farmer, I don't only encounter these wonderful tubers on my plate. From spring to fall I am out in the potato field, and that's by no means the end of it, where potatoes are concerned. With the help of the best possible storage, we can usually supply our customers with potatoes of outstanding quality right through to May. The potatoes mature during the storage process and develop a good strong flavor. No imported potatoes can compete with them. As chairman of the Bavarian potato-growers organization, I would also add: The best potatoes from the region are available all the year round and don't have to be transported long distances.

Konrad Zollner, Chairman of the Landesvereinigung der Erzeugergemeinschaften für Qualitätskartoffeln in Bayern e.V.

Organically grown potatoes

For many consumers, potatoes are the "soft drug" that introduces them to organically grown produce. There are few other foods whose flavor is so positively affected by the method of cultivation as potatoes. One reason for this is the low amount of nitrogen added to the soil through the use of organic fertilizers and previous leguminous rotation crops such as clover/grass mixes or peas. In potatoes this results in a higher dry matter content and a more intense flavor. Potatoes are an extremely demanding crop for organic farmers, because they require a great deal of care and attention throughout almost the whole year. In spring, many organic businesses begin "chitting" or "sprouting" the seed potatoes in small boxes. The aim of this is to produce a firm green shoot, which will not be damaged during planting in the ground. This gives them a head start on diseases like *Rhizoctonia solani* and the infamous potato blight. Seven to fourteen days can mean up to 30% higher production. Planting takes place in March and April.

Before the plants touch one another across the rows, they are alternately hoed and earthed up. Moving the soil up and down in this way keeps the weeds in check so they do not have to be pulled out by hand. Colorado beetles arrive at the beginning of May. They settle on the fields and in hot, dry weather they can strip a potato field bare in a few weeks. To combat the beetle larvae, which actually cause the damage, in our business we use an extract from the fruits of the Indian Neem tree. This biological pesticide destroys the appetite of the larvae. Those who want to do without pesticides entirely can also collect the larvae and beetles mechanically. In very wet weather it may be necessary to use copper fungicides, to prevent the loss of the entire crop. This fungicide has been used in viticulture for centuries. Although this substance is permitted in organic cultivation, strict conditions regarding frequency and quantity must be adhered to so that this micronutrient does not accumulate in the soil. The copper prevents the spores of the fungus from getting into the leaves and so only has a preventive effect. It can only delay the infestation of potato blight; it cannot prevent it. That would require the use of synthetic chemicals, which are not used in organic farming.

Potato varieties differ considerably in their susceptibility to potato blight. So, besides chitting, or sprouting, and the use of copper, the choice of variety is the most important preventive measure against this disease. However, what good is having a robust variety, if it does not keep well or look and taste good? Every year we test more than 20 different varieties in our fields, in order to find good, attractive, disease resistant varieties—among both old and recent, new varieties.

In our business, the variety most in demand is Linda. Linda is very popular with retailers and wholesalers, and also with customers, because it tastes good and keeps extremely well. Unfortunately it does not reliably produce the yield the farmer would like every year. Most of the old varieties like Sieglinde, La Ratte, La Bonnotte, Bamberger Hörnchen etc. are grown mainly for their flavor, their special shapes, and their color rather than for high yields or good resistance.

Our main crop potatoes are usually very early, that is, they are already ripe in August. After about three weeks on our farm they are tipped straight into wooden boxes and put into store. With good storage and by growing early potatoes under frost-protection fleece it is possible for us to supply locally grown organic potatoes 365 days a year. Up to the end of May, we have good potatoes in store from the previous year and from the beginning of June we have fresh early potatoes. So we never have to go without our favorite vegetable.

Alexander and Eva Fuchs, organic potato farmers, Schrobenhausen

Small kitchen aids

Potatoes are extremely versatile. They can be served mashed, pressed, sliced, grated, or just as they come out of the ground. For everything that goes beyond serving them in their natural form, these little kitchen aids will be a great help.

Scrubbing glove

Potatoes grow in the ground and you can clearly see this on many potatoes. For scrubbing potatoes you can use a small brush or a scrubbing glove. The glove has a rough surface, enabling you to remove encrusted earth and shoots under running water.

Peeler

Use a potato peeler on raw potatoes. The quality of the peeler will determine whether you find peeling potatoes a pleasure or a chore. With a good peeler, they almost peel themselves. When peeling potatoes it is absolutely essential to cut away any small green patches and plenty of space around them. These patches contain solanine and are poisonous, so if the patches are large, the potato should be discarded. Black and gray patches indicate damage by frost or during transport. These patches are not unhealthy, but can affect the taste and should be removed.

Potato peeling fork

Once the potatoes have been cooked, you can only peel them with a knife. To avoid burning your fingers on the hot potatoes it is best to use a special potato peeling fork. The arrangement of the tines makes sure that the potatoes do not break apart so easily.

Mashers and presses

To make a potato dough of the kind you need for such recipes as gnocchi or dumplings, you must first transform the boiled potatoes to a smooth mash. To do this, you use a masher or a potato ricer. If you do not have a potato ricer to hand, you can also use a noodle press. You should never use an electric blender for mash or potato dough. If you do, the consistency will become viscous and slimy.

Grater

For potato fritters you have to grate the raw potatoes. You must not waste any time when grating the potatoes as the flesh very quickly becomes discolored. If too much liquid collects, wrap the grated flesh in a cloth and squeeze out before continuing with the preparation.

Slicer/mandolin

For gratins you need raw slices of even thickness. If you use a knife, it takes a great deal of effort to get thin, even slices. If you do not have a food processor to do the work for you, you will have to use a potato slicer or a mandolin. Even slices also look good in potato salad.

Potato Soups and Stews

I live on good soup, not on fine words.

MOLIÈRE, 17TH-CENTURY FRENCH PLAYWRIGHT—MASTER OF SATIRICAL COMEDY

Starter or main course?

Soups were already being cooked at the time of the West Germanic tribes, probably because soup can be made from a handful of ingredients in next to no time, fills you up, and spreads a feeling of wellbeing throughout the body. Nowadays we distinguish between clear and thick soups, cream soups, vegetable soups, and stews. Stews do in fact belong with soups, even though their consistency would at first make you think otherwise. Potato soups are something for autumn and winter—their earthy, "down-home" flavor gives us a feeling of comfort and security on cold days. However, depending on how they are prepared, even earthy potato soups can have subtle nuances.

Irish potato soup with watercress

Serves 4
1¾ lb (750 g) potatoes, floury variety
2 onions
2 tbsp butter
4 cups (1 liter) vegetable stock
1 bunch watercress
4 tbsp crème fraîche
salt, pepper
1 pinch grated nutmeg

Variation
Cut 4 frankfurters, cabanossi, or other sausages for boiling in slices ½ inch (1 cm) thick and mix in after puréeing.

Peel the potatoes, rinse and cut into ½ inch (1 cm) cubes. Peel the onions and chop finely.

Heat the butter in a fairly large pan. Fry the onions over low heat until transparent, add the potatoes and pour over the vegetable stock. Cover and simmer for 25 minutes. Wash the watercress and pick off the leaves. Set a few leaves aside.

Remove a slotted spoonful of potatoes from the pan, drain, and set aside. Add the watercress to the pan and purée everything finely with a hand blender. Stir in the crème fraîche and bring briefly to a boil. Season the soup to taste with salt and pepper. Return the spoonful of potatoes to the pan. Pour the soup into warmed bowls, sprinkle with a little nutmeg, and garnish with the remaining watercress leaves.

Cream of zucchini and potato soup with fresh cilantro

Peel the onion and garlic, chop finely, and fry lightly together with the butter in a wide sauté pan. Trim and wash the zucchini and cut in slices. Add to the pan and fry briefly. Peel the potatoes, rinse, dice coarsely, and add to the pan. Season with salt and pepper. Pour over the vegetable stock and bring slowly to a boil. Stir in the crème fraîche. Cover and simmer over medium heat for about 25 minutes. Meanwhile, wash the cilantro, pick off the leaves and set a few aside. Chop the remaining leaves fairly fine. Purée the soup with a hand blender, season to taste with salt and pepper, and mix in the chopped cilantro. Pour the soup into warmed bowls and sprinkle with the remaining cilantro leaves.

Serves 4
1 onion
1 garlic clove
2 tbsp butter
14 oz (400 g) small zucchini
1¼ lb (600 g) potatoes, floury variety
4 cups (1 liter) vegetable stock
3 tbsp crème fraîche
salt, pepper
½ bunch fresh cilantro

Cream of potato and fennel soup

Serves 4
2 onions
2 fennel bulbs
14 oz (400 g) potatoes, floury variety
2 tbsp olive oil
¼ cup (60 ml) aniseed-flavored pastis, such as ouzo
4 cups (1 liter) vegetable stock
2 tbsp pine nuts
scant ½ cup (100 ml) light cream
salt, pepper
lemon juice

Peel the onions and chop finely. Trim the fennel bulbs, rinse, and chop coarsely. Wash the fennel stems and leaves, chop finely, and set aside. Peel the potatoes and dice coarsely. Heat the olive oil in a pan and fry the onions lightly until soft. Add the fennel and the potatoes and fry briefly. Flavor with the pastis and pour over the vegetable stock. Cover and simmer for 30 minutes.
Toast the pine nuts in a dry pan until golden brown. Add the cream to the soup and purée with a hand blender. Season to taste with salt, pepper, and lemon juice. Pour into warmed bowls and sprinkle with the toasted pine nuts and chopped fennel leaves before serving.

Red potato cream soup with smoked trout

Serves 4
11 oz (300 g) beet
generous 1 lb (500 g) potatoes, floury variety
2 shallots
3 tbsp butter
4 cups (1 liter) vegetable stock
3 tbsp crème fraîche
½ bunch dill
7 oz (200 g) smoked trout fillets
salt, pepper
¼ tsp cayenne pepper
a little lemon juice

Boil the unpeeled beet in just enough water to cover them for about 40 minutes until tender, and the potatoes in a second pan for about 30 minutes, or until soft. Peel the shallots and chop finely. Peel the potatoes when cool and cut in rough cubes. Rinse the beet in cold water, peel, and dice coarsely.
Melt 2 tablespoons of butter in a pan and fry the shallots gently until transparent. Add the potatoes and beet, and fry briefly with the shallots. Pour over the vegetable stock and bring to a boil. Purée finely with a hand blender and stir in the crème fraîche. Cover and simmer for 10 minutes.
Meanwhile, wash the dill, pat dry, and chop coarsely. Divide the trout fillets into bite-size pieces and fry briefly in the remaining butter. Season the soup to taste with salt, pepper, cayenne pepper, and lemon juice. Pour into warmed bowls, scatter over the trout pieces, and sprinkle with dill.

Tip
In summer this soup is also delicious served chilled, with the smoked trout simply added cold.

Cream of potato soup with porcini mushrooms

SERVES 4
1 medium onion
2 tbsp butter
1¾ lb (750 g) potatoes, floury variety
4 cups (1 liter) vegetable stock
7 oz (200 g) fresh porcini mushrooms
3½ tbsp dry white wine
5 tbsp crème fraîche
salt, pepper
1 pinch grated nutmeg

Made with fresh mushrooms, this is a wonderful soup for the fall; it can also be made with dried porcini mushrooms.

Peel the onion and chop finely. Melt half the butter in a pan and fry the onion gently until transparent. Peel the potatoes, rinse, dice coarsely, and add to the pan. Pour over the vegetable stock, bring to a boil, cover, and simmer for 20 minutes, or until soft.
Trim the mushrooms, wash briefly under running water, wipe dry, and cut in small pieces. Fry in the remaining butter for 5 minutes, and season to taste with salt and pepper.
Add half the fried mushrooms to the soup, and purée with a hand blender. Stir in the white wine and crème fraîche, and bring to a boil. Season to taste with salt, pepper, and nutmeg. Serve the soup in warmed bowls sprinkled with the remaining mushrooms.

TIP
Alternatively, you can use 1¾ oz (50 g) dried porcini mushrooms, which must be soaked in hot water. The soaking water can then be strained and stirred into the soup, giving it an even richer flavor.

Sweet and sour oyster mushroom and potato soup

SERVES 4
2 stalks lemongrass
1 piece galangal, about 1 inch (2.5 cm)
3 kaffir lime leaves
3 shallots
4 cups (1 liter) chicken stock
14 oz (400 g) small potatoes
12 small oyster mushrooms
½ bunch garlic (or Chinese) chives
4 tbsp fish sauce

Remove the coarse outer layers of the lemongrass and chop finely. Peel and slice the galangal. Wash the kaffir lime leaves and cut in narrow strips. Peel and quarter the shallots. Put all the above in a pan and pour over the chicken stock. Bring to a boil and simmer for 30 minutes. Meanwhile, peel, rinse, and quarter the potatoes. Briefly wash the oyster mushrooms under running water and wipe dry. Briefly wash the garlic chives and cut in longish pieces. Strain the stock into a clean pan, add the potatoes, and simmer for just under 20 minutes. Add the oyster mushrooms after 10 minutes, and finally sprinkle with the garlic chives. Flavor the soup to taste with fish sauce. Pour into warmed bowls and serve.

Potato and chestnut soup with halibut

Peel the onion and garlic and chop finely. Peel the potatoes, rinse, and dice coarsely.

Melt the butter in a pan, and fry the onion and garlic until transparent. Add the potatoes and chestnuts and pour over the vegetable stock. Bring to a boil, cover, and simmer over low heat for 20 minutes, or until soft.

Meanwhile, rinse the chives and cut in thin rings. Remove the skin from the halibut and cut in bite-size pieces.

Purée the soup with a hand blender. Mix in the cream cheese and bring to a boil. Season to taste with salt, pepper, and lemon juice. Add the halibut and leave to simmer for a few minutes over low heat. Serve the soup in warmed bowls sprinkled with the chives.

Serves 4

1 large onion
1 garlic clove
generous 1 lb (500 g) potatoes
2 tbsp butter
9 oz (250 g) chestnuts, boiled and peeled
4 cups (1 liter) vegetable stock
½ bunch chives
9 oz (250 g) smoked halibut
scant ½ cup (100 g) cream cheese
salt, white pepper
1 tsp lemon juice

Franconian potato soup

SERVES 4
5½ oz (150 g) about 11 sliced bacon strips
2 packs soup vegetables
1 large onion
1¼ lb (600 g) potatoes, floury variety
2 tbsp oil
4 cups (1 liter) meat stock
½ bunch chives
salt, pepper
1 tsp dried marjoram
optional herbs

Remove any rind from the bacon and dice small. Prepare the soup vegetables, and cut in small pieces. Peel the onion and chop finely. Peel and rinse the potatoes, and dice coarsely.

Heat the oil in a pan and fry the bacon until tender. Add the onion and other vegetables and fry lightly for 5 minutes. Add the potatoes and pour over the meat stock. Bring to a boil, cover, lower the heat, and continue to cook for 25 minutes, or until soft. Meanwhile wash the chives and cut in thin rings. Season the soup to taste with salt, pepper, and marjoram. Reduce the potatoes to a smooth mash using a potato masher or potato ricer and season again. Serve in warmed bowls, sprinkled with the chives and any favorite herb.

Cream of potato and asparagus soup with Parmesan

Peel and rinse the potatoes, and cut in ½ inch (1 cm) cubes. Wash and peel the asparagus, and cut off the woody ends. Cut the stems in pieces ½ inch (1 cm) long, and set the tips aside.
Peel the onion and chop finely. Melt the butter in a wide sauté pan and fry the onion gently. Add the diced potato and asparagus pieces and fry briefly. Season to taste with salt, pepper, and nutmeg. Wash the chervil, pick off the leaves. Set a few leaves aside. Chop the remainder roughly, and add to the pan. Pour over the vegetable stock, cover, and simmer for 25 minutes.
Meanwhile blanch the asparagus tips in boiling salted water, rinse under ice-cold water, and leave to drain thoroughly. Purée the soup with a hand blender. Stir in the crème fraîche and grated Parmesan, bring to a boil, and season to taste with salt, pepper, and lemon juice. Serve the soup in warmed bowls, garnished with the blanched asparagus tips and the remaining chervil leaves.

SERVES 4
14 oz (400 g) potatoes, floury variety
generous 1 lb (500 g) green asparagus
1 small onion
2 tbsp butter
1 pinch grated nutmeg
1 handful chervil
4 cups (1 liter) vegetable stock
4 tbsp crème fraîche
3 tbsp grated Parmesan
salt, pepper
lemon juice

TIP
White asparagus can be used instead of green.

Normandy potato and apple soup with cider

SERVES 4
2 medium onions
2 large apples, e.g. Elstar
2 tbsp butter
1¼ lb (600 g) potatoes, floury variety
3 cups (¾ liter) vegetable stock
generous ¾ cup (200 ml) hard cider
scant ½ cup (100 ml) crème fraîche
1 tsp apple vinegar
½ bunch chives
salt, pepper

A traditional northern France specialty from the home of cider and crème fraîche.

Peel the onions and chop finely. Peel and quarter the apples, remove the cores, and chop roughly. Melt the butter in a wide sauté pan and fry the onion and apples until soft. Meanwhile, peel and rinse the potatoes, chop into rough cubes and add to the pan. Pour over the vegetable stock and cider, and bring to a boil. Cool slightly then stir in the crème fraîche, cover, and simmer for about 25 minutes.

Season the soup to taste with salt and pepper and add apple vinegar to taste. Wash the chives, cut in fine rings, and mix half into the soup. Serve the soup in warmed bowls sprinkled with the remaining chives.

Potato and mushroom goulash

SERVES 4
2 red bell peppers
1 onion
2 garlic cloves
generous 1 lb (500 g) mushrooms
1¾ lb (750 g) potatoes, waxy variety
3 tbsp oil
3 tbsp tomato paste
1 tbsp mild ground paprika
1¼ tsp cayenne pepper
salt, pepper
1 tsp marjoram, fresh or dried
4 cups (1 liter) vegetable stock
2 scallions

Trim and wash the bell peppers and dice small. Peel the onions and garlic and chop finely. Wash the mushrooms briefly under running water, wipe dry, and cut in halves or quarters, depending on the size. Peel and rinse the potatoes, and cut in cubes.

Heat the oil in a wide sauté pan and fry the onions and garlic until tender. Mix in the tomato paste and season with ground paprika, salt, pepper, cayenne pepper, and marjoram. Add the peppers, potatoes, and mushrooms to the pan. Pour over the vegetable stock, bring to a boil, cover and simmer for 20 minutes over low heat. Taste the goulash and add extra seasoning if necessary. Trim and wash the scallions, chop finely, and sprinkle over the goulash to serve.

VARIATION

Cut frankfurters, cabanossi, landjäger, or other boiling sausages, in small pieces and add to the goulash around 10 minutes before the end of the cooking time.

Potato and vegetable soup with Parmesan crackers

Serves 4
1¾ cups (200 g) grated Parmesan
1 onion
1 garlic clove
11 oz (300 g) early potatoes, predominantly waxy variety
1 small zucchini
generous 1 lb (500 g) green asparagus
¾ cup (100 g) needle, or very narrow, green beans
2 tbsp olive oil
4 cups (1 liter) vegetable stock
1 bunch basil
salt, pepper

Preheat the oven to 355 °F (180 °C). Line a baking sheet with baking paper. Arrange the grated Parmesan on the sheet in small piles, flatten a little, and bake in the oven for 10 minutes. Take out the crackers and leave to cool.
Peel the onion and garlic and chop finely. Peel, rinse, and dice the potatoes. Wash and slice the zucchini. Wash the asparagus, peel the bottom third, and cut the stems in pieces. Trim and wash the beans. Heat the olive oil in a large pan and lightly brown the onion and garlic. Add the vegetables and potatoes and season with salt and pepper. Pour over the vegetable stock, bring to a boil, cover, and simmer over low heat for 20 minutes. Meanwhile, wash the basil, pick off the leaves, pat dry, and chop roughly. Taste the soup and season again if necessary. Pour into warmed bowls, sprinkle with the basil, and serve with the Parmesan crackers.

Bean and potato stew

Serves 4
generous 1 lb (500 g) green beans
1 onion
1 carrot
1 small leek
½ cup (100 g) diced celery root
2 tbsp butter
1 tbsp all-purpose flour
4 cups (1 liter) vegetable stock
1 bunch savory
1¼ lb (600 g) potatoes, waxy variety
2 tbsp herb vinegar
generous ¾ cup (200 ml) sour cream
salt, pepper

This stew is a traditional, wholesome dish from Luxembourg.

Trim and wash the beans, and cut diagonally in pieces about ¾ inch (2 cm) long. Peel the onion, carrot, and cut into small dice. Trim and wash the leek and cut in thin rounds. Heat the butter in a pan and lightly fry the onion, carrot, leek, and celery root.
Add the beans to the pan, dust with the flour, season with salt and pepper, and pour over the vegetable stock. Wash the savory, do not chop, but add the whole bunch to the pan, cover, and simmer for 10 minutes. Peel and rinse the potatoes, and cut in ¾ inch (2 cm) cubes. Mix with the beans and cook everything for a further 15 minutes until tender.
Remove the savory bunch. Season with plenty of salt, pepper, and herb vinegar to taste. Lastly, stir in the sour cream, but do not allow to boil, otherwise it will curdle.

Spanish potato and meat casserole with red wine

Serves 4
generous 1 lb (500 g) pork fillet
1¼ lb (600 g) potatoes, waxy variety
1 large onion
2 garlic cloves
3 tbsp olive oil
2 tbsp tomato paste
1 small, dried chile
1 tsp mild ground paprika
salt, pepper
2 cups (½ liter) meat stock
2 cups (½ liter) Rioja (Spanish red wine)
½ bunch parsley

Cut the pork in bite-size cubes. Peel and rinse the potatoes, and cut in cubes of the same size. Peel the onion and garlic and chop finely. Heat the olive oil in a wide sauté pan, brown the meat well, and remove from the pan. Then add the potatoes to the pan and brown briefly. Return the meat to the pan and add the onion and garlic. Stir in the tomato paste and add the chile. Season with ground paprika, salt, and pepper. Pour over the meat stock, cover, and simmer for 30 minutes. Add the red wine and cook for a further 15 minutes. Wash the parsley, chop roughly, and stir in.

Tip
It is best to drink the same red wine that you used in the cooking of this dish.

Dutch Hutspot with beef tenderloin

Serves 4
1¾ lb (800 g) beef tenderloin
3 cups (¾ liter) meat stock
generous 1 lb (500 g) carrots
3 onions
1¾ lb (800 g) potatoes, floury variety
1 bunch chives
2 tbsp butter
salt, pepper

This dish is said to date back to the year 1574. When the Spanish fled from the city of Leiden, so the story goes, they left behind a pot containing a dish of carrots, onions, and potatoes. This stew was called "hutspot."

Put the meat in a pan and barely cover with meat stock. Cover the pan and cook for 30 minutes over medium heat. Meanwhile peel, rinse, and slice the carrots. Peel the onions and cut in thin rings. Peel, rinse, and quarter the potatoes.
Add the vegetables to the pan, cover, and cook over medium heat for a further 30 minutes until tender. Wash the chives and chop small. Remove the meat from the pan and keep warm. Mash the contents of the pan, while mixing in the butter and chives, and season generously with salt and pepper. Cut the meat in slices ½ inch (1 cm) thick and arrange on top of the mash.

Vichyssoise — chilled leek and potato soup

Serves 4
500 g (generous 1 lb) potatoes, floury variety
4 fairly thin leeks, white parts
3 tbsp butter
4 cups (1 liter) vegetable stock
1 pinch nutmeg
scant ⅔ cup (150 ml) sour cream
salt, pepper

This classic, elegant soup is a refreshing treat on hot summer days.

Peel, rinse, and dice the potatoes. Trim and wash the leeks and cut the white part only in rounds, discard the green. Melt the butter in a pan and lightly soften the leek along with the potatoes but do not allow to brown. Pour over the vegetable stock and simmer for 25 minutes. Then purée and season with salt, pepper, and nutmeg. Allow the soup to cool completely and mix in the sour cream with a hand blender before serving. Serve chilled.

Oriental potato stew

Serves 4
1½ cups (300 g) pinto beans
2 onions, 2 garlic cloves
3 tbsp olive oil
2 cups (500 g) ground beef
2 tbsp tomato paste
juice of 2 limes
1 tsp ground cinnamon
6 cups (1½ liters) meat stock
500 g (generous 1 lb) small potatoes, waxy variety
generous 1 lb (500 g) tomatoes
½ bunch fresh mint, salt & pepper

Soak the pinto beans overnight in cold water. Peel the onions and garlic and chop finely. Heat the oil in a pan and brown the ground beef with the onion and garlic. Stir in the tomato paste, lime juice, and cinnamon. Add the stock and bring to a boil, cover, and simmer over low heat for 1 hour.
Meanwhile, peel the potatoes and add to the pan after 30 minutes. Scald the tomatoes, discard the skins, chop the flesh coarsely, and mix in. Wash the mint, pick off the leaves, and chop coarsely. Season the stew to taste and fold in the mint before serving.

Potato curry with yellow lentils

Serves 4
2 garlic cloves
1 piece ginger, c. 1¼ inch (3 cm)
1 onion, 3 tbsp olive oil
2 tsp mustard seeds, 1 chile
3 tsp ground cumin
2 tbsp curry powder
1 tsp ground turmeric
1¼ lb (600 g) potatoes, floury variety
1¼ cups (250 g) yellow lentils
14 oz (400 g) can tomatoes
generous 2 cups (1¼ liters) vegetable stock
4 tbsp crème fraîche
1 tbsp lemon juice, salt, pepper
few cilantro sprigs

Peel the garlic, ginger, and onion and chop finely. Heat the oil in a wide sauté pan. Toast the mustard seeds in the oil for 30 seconds. Add the onion and fry until transparent. Add the garlic, ginger, chile, cumin, curry powder, and turmeric and cook for a few more minutes.
Peel the potatoes, cut in rough cubes and add to the pan. Rinse the lentils and add to the pan with the tomatoes and the juice from the can. Pour over the vegetable stock, bring to a boil, cover and simmer for 20 minutes, until the lentils are soft. Add the crème fraîche, and season with salt, pepper, and lemon juice to taste. Garnish with sprigs of fresh cilantro.

Tip
Cut two chicken breast fillets in small pieces, fry lightly until the meat is cooked through, and mix in.

Cream of potato soup with cod

SERVES 4
1 large onion
1 garlic clove
1¾ lb (750 g) potatoes, floury variety
2 tbsp butter
4 cups (1 liter) vegetable stock
½ bunch chives
9 oz (250 g) smoked cod
5 tbsp sour cream
1 tsp lemon juice
salt, pepper

Peel the onion and garlic and chop finely. Peel and rinse the potatoes, and dice roughly.

Melt the butter in a pan and fry the onion and garlic until transparent. Add the potatoes and pour over the vegetable stock. Bring to a boil, cover, and cook for 20 minutes over low heat.

Meanwhile, wash the chives and cut in thin rings. Remove the skin from the cod and divide in pieces. Purée the soup with a hand blender and mix in the sour cream. Add the cod and allow the flavor to develop briefly over low heat. Season the soup with salt, pepper, and lemon juice to taste. Pour into warmed bowls and sprinkle with chives.

Potato and vegetable stew with pork

SERVES 4
1¼ lb (600 g) pork shoulder
2 onions
1 garlic clove
about ½ cup (100 g) diced celery root
3 tbsp oil
4 allspice berries
1 bay leaf
4 cups (1 liter) meat stock
generous 1 lb (500 g) potatoes, predominantly waxy variety
3–4 medium (500 g) carrots
1 bunch scallions
salt, pepper

Cut the meat in bite-size cubes. Peel the onions and dice small. Peel the garlic and chop finely.

Heat the oil in a casserole, brown the meat fiercely on all sides, and season with salt and pepper. Add the onions, diced celery root, and garlic and fry briefly with the meat. Add the allspice and bay leaf and pour over the meat stock. Cover the pan and cook over low heat for 40 minutes until tender. Meanwhile, peel the potatoes and carrots, rinse, and cut in thin slices. Mix with the meat and cook for a further 30 minutes. Trim and wash the scallions, cut in rings, and stir in 5 minutes before the end of cooking time. Season the stew with salt and pepper to taste. Remove the bay leaf before serving.

Hungarian potato and bell pepper stew

Peel and rinse the potatoes, and cut in about ¾ inch (2 cm) cubes. Trim and wash the bell peppers, and dice small. Discard the rind from the bacon and dice small. Peel the onion and garlic and chop finely.

Heat the oil in a pan over low heat and fry the bacon gently. Add the onions and garlic and fry until transparent. Stir in the tomato paste and season well with salt, pepper, and ground paprika. Add the potatoes and pour over the meat stock. Cover the pan, bring to a boil and simmer for 20 minutes over low heat. After 10 minutes mix in the diced bell peppers.

Wash the chives and cut in thin rings. Season again to taste if necessary, and serve sprinkled with the chives.

Serves 4

generous 1 lb (500 g) potatoes, waxy variety
2 red bell peppers
3½ oz (100 g) smoked slab bacon
1 tbsp oil
1 large onion
1 garlic clove
2 tbsp tomato paste
1 pinch medium hot ground paprika
4 cups (1 liter) meat stock
1 bunch chives
salt, pepper

Potato terrine with artichokes

Serves 4–6
2 onions
5 garlic cloves
1 tbsp butter
14 oz (400 g) can or jar artichoke hearts and/or bottoms
1½ cups (150 g) black olives, pitted
generous ¾ cup (200 g) sour cream
1 cup (100 g) grated Parmesan
1¾ lb (800 g) potatoes, waxy variety
grated nutmeg
5½ oz (150 g) smoked bacon in slices
salt, pepper

Peel the onions and 2 garlic cloves and chop finely. Melt the butter in a pan and fry the onions and garlic until soft. Drain the artichoke hearts thoroughly and cut in strips.

Peel the remaining garlic cloves and chop finely. Roughly chop the olives. Mix both with the sour cream and the Parmesan, and season to taste with salt and pepper. Peel and rinse the potatoes, and slice thinly. Mix the strips of artichoke with the potatoes and the fried onions. Season with salt, pepper, and nutmeg.

Preheat the oven to 400 °F (200 °C). Line the bottom of a terrine or loaf pan with half the slices of bacon. Spread with one third of the potato mixture, then one third of the cream mixture. Add alternate layers of potato and cream mixtures, until all the ingredients have been used up. Then cover with a layer of bacon slices and bake in the preheated oven (middle shelf) for 1 hour. Remove from the oven, allow to cool, then tip out and serve with a herb vinaigrette if desired.

Bouillon potatoes with Tafelspitz (prime boiled beef) and apple and horseradish sauce

Serves 4
1 onion
1 pack vegetables for soup
2 lb 10 oz (1.2 kg) fresh brisket (or silverside) beef
1 bay leaf
1 tsp peppercorns
14 oz (400 g) apples, e.g. Topaz or Braeburn
5½ oz (150 g) fresh horseradish, or from a jar
1 cup (250 g) sour cream
1 pinch sugar
14 oz (400 g) potatoes, waxy variety
4 medium (300 g) carrots
2 thin leeks
optional herbs
salt, pepper

Peel and quarter the onion. Prepare the soup vegetables and chop small. Rinse the beef and pat dry. Pour 8 cups (2 liters) of water into a deep pan or Dutch oven, add the onion and vegetables and bring to a boil with the bay leaf, peppercorns, and salt. Add the beef, cover and cook over low heat sufficient to maintain a gentle rolling boil for 1½ hours until tender. Check from time to time.

Meanwhile, for the sauce, peel and quarter the apples, remove the core and grate coarsely. Peel the horseradish, grate, and mix with the apples and sour cream. Season with salt, pepper, and sugar and refrigerate until serving.

About 30 minutes before the end of the cooking time for the beef, take out about 2 cups (500 ml) of the cooking liquid, pour through a strainer into a second pan and bring to a boil. Meanwhile, peel and rinse the potatoes and carrots, and dice coarsely. Trim and wash the leeks, and cut in rings. Add the potatoes and carrots to the liquid, cover, and simmer for 15 minutes. Add the leeks and any favorite herb and simmer for a further 5 minutes, then remove the bay leaf. Remove the beef from the pan, cut in finger-thick slices, arrange on warmed plates and pour over a little of the liquid. Remove the vegetables from the liquid with a slotted spoon, allow to drain, and add to the beef. Serve with the apple and horseradish sauce.

Wide Range of Salads

You need four men to make a salad; a generous man for the oil, a miser for the vinegar, a wise man for the salt, and a fool for the pepper.
François Coppée, 19th-century French poet, dramatist, and novelist

More than just a salad

There have been many arguments about what a good potato salad should taste like. Some swear by warm potato salad, others mix in mayonnaise, or use purple potatoes to bring a little color into it. There are few other dishes where regional preferences are so marked and so passionately defended. All the same, you may perhaps find some kind of inspiration in our salads that will broaden the horizons of your salad bowl.

Swabian potato salad

Serves 4–6
2¼ lb (1 kg) potatoes, waxy variety, as evenly sized as possible
2 onions
generous ¾ cup (200 ml) stock (meat or vegetable stock, according to preference)
6–8 tbsp apple vinegar
8 tbsp sunflower oil
1 bunch chives
2 radishes
salt, pepper

This is my Swabian grandmother's recipe. For me, it's the best potato salad in the world. It is eaten with roasts, schnitzels, sausages, or the Swabian specialty—roasted pasta pockets.

Wash the potatoes thoroughly, put in a pan and just cover with water, and boil for 20–25 minutes, or until tender but still firm. Meanwhile peel the onions and dice very small. Peel the hot potatoes and slice thinly into a bowl. Add the onions. Bring the stock and vinegar together to a boil and pour the hot stock over the potatoes. Season with salt and pepper. Pour over the sunflower oil, mix gently, and leave for 30 minutes to let the flavors develop. Wash the chives, pat dry with paper towels, cut in thin rings, and fold in before serving. Cut the radishes in thin slices and use to decorate the salad.

Tip
In summer, you can give it a refreshing taste by mixing in thin slices of cucumber.

Potato salad with salmon trout and mint

Serves 4
2¼ lb (1 kg) small potatoes, waxy variety
½ bunch dill
½ bunch mint
½ cup (125 g) sour cream
1 tbsp white balsamic vinegar
1 garlic clove
14 oz (400 g) smoked salmon trout fillets
salt, pepper

Wash the potatoes thoroughly, put in a pan with just enough water to cover, and boil with the lid on for about 20 minutes, or until tender but still firm. Wash the dill and mint under running water, pat dry, pick off the mint leaves, and snip the dill fronds. In a salad bowl, mix together the sour cream and balsamic vinegar. Peel the garlic, crush with a garlic press or the flat blade of a knife, and stir into the mixture. Season the dressing with salt and pepper to taste.
Halve or quarter the potatoes, depending on the size, mix with the dressing and leave for 10 minutes to let the flavors develop. Divide the salmon trout into bite-size pieces. Arrange the potatoes and salmon trout on four plates and garnish with the mint and dill.

North German potato salad

SERVES 4–6
2¼ lb (1 kg) potatoes as evenly sized as possible, waxy variety
1 large onion
5 pickled gherkins
4 tbsp vinegar
½ cup (125 g) sour cream
1 tsp medium hot mustard
1 bunch chives
salt, pepper

Wash the potatoes, put in a pan with just enough water to cover. Boil with the lid on for about 20–25 minutes, or until tender but still firm. Meanwhile peel the onion and chop finely. Dice the gherkins small. Drain the potatoes, peel, and cut in cubes of about ¾ inch (2 cm). In a bowl, mix the potatoes with the onion and gherkins.

In a small bowl, mix the vinegar with the sour cream and mustard, season to taste with salt and pepper, and add to the potatoes. Mix together and leave for 20 minutes to let the flavors develop. Wash the chives, pat dry with paper towels, cut in thin rings, and mix in before serving.

American potato salad with avocado and vegetables

SERVES 6
1¾ lb (800 g) potatoes, waxy variety
4 medium ribs, 9 oz (250 g) celery
2 avocados
3 tbsp lemon juice
1 red bell pepper
5 tbsp mayonnaise
5 tbsp white wine vinegar
2 tbsp oil
1 pinch sugar
¼ tsp cayenne pepper
salt, pepper

Wash the potatoes, put in a pan with just enough water to cover, and boil with the lid on for about 30 minutes, or until tender but still firm.

Meanwhile trim and wash the celery, slice, and tip into a large bowl. Cut the avocados in half, pit, scoop the flesh from the skin, and dice small. Drizzle immediately with lemon juice so that the flesh does not turn brown, and add to the bowl. Trim and wash the bell pepper, dice small, and add to the bowl.

Drain the potatoes and allow to cool a little. Then peel, cut in cubes of about ¾ inch (2 cm) and add to the bowl. With a hand whisk, beat together the mayonnaise, vinegar, sugar, cayenne pepper, and salt and pepper to taste. Pour the dressing over the salad ingredients, mix in gently and leave for 20 minutes to let the flavors develop.

TIP

Avocados should be ripe and soft. If they are still hard, wrap them in newspaper and leave them to ripen at room temperature for 2 to 3 days. You can tell that the fruit is ripe, if the flesh yields under the pressure of your fingers.

Potato and carrot salad with raisins

Wash the potatoes, put in a pan with barely enough water to cover, and boil with the lid on for about 20—25 minutes, or until tender but still firm. Peel the carrots and dice small. Cook for 5 minutes in boiling salted water, rinse in ice-cold water, and drain well. Peel the potatoes and cut in ¾ inch (2 cm) cubes. Put them in a bowl with the diced carrots.
Trim and wash the scallions, cut in thin rings, and add to the bowl along with the raisins. Make a dressing from the orange juice, olive oil, salt, and pepper. Pour over the salad and mix in. Cover and refrigerate for 20 minutes to let the flavors develop, then season again to taste if necessary. Potatoes absorb a lot of seasoning.

Serves 4
1¾ lb (800 g) potatoes, waxy variety
generous 1 lb (500 g) carrots
2 scallions
½ cup (50 g) raisins
juice of 1 medium orange
6 tbsp olive oil
salt, pepper

Potato and radicchio salad with honey dressing

Scrub the potatoes well, put in a pan and cover with water. Bring to a boil, with the lid on, and simmer for 20 minutes, or until tender but still firm. Drain and allow to cool.
Meanwhile, trim the mushrooms, wash briefly under running water, dry with paper towels, and cut in quarters. Heat 2 tablespoons of the oil in a large pan, brown the mushrooms quickly over high heat, and sprinkle with oregano. In a large salad bowl mix together the apple vinegar, honey, salt, and pepper until the salt has completely dissolved. Then beat in the remaining olive oil with a hand whisk to make a creamy dressing.
Cut the unpeeled potatoes into fairly thick slices, mix with the dressing, and leave for at least 15 minutes to let the flavors develop. Trim and wash the scallions, and cut in rings. Cut the radicchio in quarters and then in fairly broad strips, wash, and drain. Mix in with the potatoes, together with the mushrooms and scallions. Check the seasoning before serving.

Serves 4
1¾ lb (800 g) potatoes, waxy variety
9 oz (250 g) cremini (chestnut) mushrooms
6 tbsp olive oil
1 tsp oregano
4 tbsp apple vinegar
1 tbsp honey
3 scallions
1 small radicchio
salt, pepper

Potato salad with matjes herrings, beet, and apple

SERVES 4
generous 1 lb (500 g) potatoes, waxy variety
about 3 medium, 14 oz (400 g) beet
2 eggs
1 medium onion
2 gherkins
1 fairly sharp apple, e.g. Granny Smith
a little lemon juice
4 matjes fillets
1 bunch dill
5 tbsp oil, 5 tbsp vinegar
1 tsp sweet mustard
salt, pepper

Wash the potatoes and beet and place in two separate pans with just enough water to cover. Boil with the lids on for about 30 minutes, or until tender but still firm. Boil the eggs for 10 minutes, rinse in cold water and peel. Peel the onion and chop finely. Dice the gherkins small. Peel the apple, remove the core, dice small, and drizzle with lemon juice so that the flesh does not turn brown. Drain the potatoes and beet, allow to cool a little, peel, and dice small. Tip into a bowl, together with the prepared ingredients, except the eggs.

Rinse the matjes fillets in cold water, pat dry, cut in small pieces, and add to the bowl. Wash the dill, snip off the fronds, and chop finely. Using a hand whisk, mix the oil, vinegar, and mustard, together thoroughly with salt and pepper to taste, and pour over the salad. Mix well and leave for 30 minutes to let the flavors develop. Cut the eggs in quarters and use to garnish the salad.

Mediterranean potato salad with cherry tomatoes, olives, and capers

SERVES 4
1¾ lb (800 g) small potatoes, waxy variety
4 tbsp white balsamic vinegar
1 pinch sugar
1 tsp Dijon mustard
8 tbsp olive oil
1 garlic clove
9 oz (250 g) cherry tomatoes
5 tbsp capers, drained
1 tsp thyme
1 cup (100 g) black olives, pitted
salt, pepper

Scrub the potatoes well, put in a pan with a little water and boil for 25 minutes, or until tender but still firm. Drain and allow to cool. In a large salad bowl, mix together the balsamic vinegar, sugar, and mustard with salt and pepper to taste. Beat in the olive oil with a hand whisk to give a creamy dressing.

Peel the garlic, crush in a garlic press, or with the flat blade of a knife and mix into the bowl. Wash the cherry tomatoes, cut in half, and add to the bowl, along with the capers, thyme, and olives. Cut the potatoes in half or quarters, depending on the size, add to the bowl, mix, and leave for 10 minutes to let the flavors develop.

Herbs and spices

Potatoes have a very delicate flavor and, unless you are using a purple variety, they are also a delicate color. Spices, herbs, and edible plants will enable you to give any dish new nuances of taste and color. What is more, many of these plants are not only tasty and attractive to look at, they also have health-giving properties, which you can also pass on just by mixing them into the dishes you prepare. However it is advisable to wash all fresh herbs before using and grow your own if possible. Of course there are many other herbs and spices that can be combined with potatoes—this small selection represents my favorites to go with potatoes.

Arugula

Arugula came to Europe via the Mediterranean area from the Middle East. Chopped finely and mixed in, it gives potato salad more of a spicy flavor. In some English-speaking countries, arugula is known as "rocket," or by its Italian name "rucola." It is advisable to wash arugula before using and home-grown means it is really fresh.

Basil

Basil is so closely associated in our minds with tomatoes and mozzarella, that only a few people are aware that it originates from the Indian subcontinent. There are several types of this popular herb, such as cinnamon basil, bush basil, and the purple leaf variety opal basil, as well as lemon, anise, and clove basils. Aromatic basil is especially good with Mediterranean dishes, but has a very dominant flavor and should therefore be used with care.

Basil can be grown on any windowsill. Daisies and nasturtiums are good for adding a touch of color to salads.

Beet shoots

Beet shoots can be grown from seed at home on a windowsill in 7—10 days. The shoots are eaten raw and their red color makes them ideal for serving with quark and potatoes boiled in their skins.

Chervil

Chervil has a very delicate flavor, which makes it perfect for enhancing the taste of food. Only ever pick the young, delicate leaves and never cook them with the other ingredients. Chervil should only be sprinkled on soups or potatoes boiled in their skins at the last minute.

Chives

Chives like fairly cool, moist conditions. When it gets too warm, they quickly start to look sorry for themselves. Their tangy flavor, which is a bit like that of fresh onions, and slight sharpness makes chives excellent for sprinkling on soups and potato salad. Chives should not be heated, as that causes a large part of the vitamins to be lost. Chive flowers are also edible and and good for decorating salads.

Cilantro

People either like or hate cilantro, which are the leaves and stems of the coriander plant. This herb, known as coriander in Europe, has leaves that give off a pungent smell and have a flavor that for many is somewhat of an acquired taste. However, in contrast, the taste and smell of ripe coriander seeds is deliciously sweet and spicy, and the ground dried seeds are used extensively. Fresh cilantro is particularly popular in Indian cuisine.

Cumin

Cumin is found almost everywhere. It can be subdivided into cumin and black cumin. The former is mainly used in Middle-Eastern and Asian dishes, while black cumin is often used as a flavoring in breads and cheeses. Cumin seeds are excellent for preventing flatulence and stomach cramps and are mixed into foods that are hard to digest because of their prophylactic effect.

Daisies

Daisies grow in lawns and meadows all over Europe and also in Asia Minor and North America. Although they have a sweetish scent, they taste slightly sour and bitter. They have a very stimulating effect on the metabolism, and consequently people also keep them in their medicine cabinets at home to stimulate the liver and gall bladder. In the kitchen, daisies make wonderful edible decorations. Sprinkled over potato salad, they make it look very fresh and spring-like.

Fenugreek

It has been said that if people knew what there was in it, they would pay its weight in gold. It therefore comes as no surprise that it is used as a health-giving flavoring in many Middle-Eastern and Far-Eastern dishes. Ground fenugreek seed is also one of the main ingredients in curry powders.

Garlic

Garlic was known to the ancient Egyptians, Greeks, Chinese, and Indians. It was used both for food and as a medicine. Garlic oil has an antibiotic effect and also includes trace elements, selenium, and vitamins. There are different varieties of garlic, some stronger and hotter than others. Garlic is an essential ingredient of dishes like moussaka and it spices up salad dressings. Incidentally, you can

reduce the unmistakable smell somewhat by removing the shoot—the little green center of the garlic clove.

Lavender

Lavender originates from the Mediterranean region of southern Europe. It particularly enjoys warm, dry conditions and does not like getting its feet wet. Lavender should be drunk as an infusion to counter internal anxiety and stress. The young shoots can be used to flavor stews, while small lavender blossoms look pretty on mashed potato.

Marjoram

Marjoram comes from North Africa. It has a strong, unmistakable flavor, so it is not used much in light dishes but more in stews and bakes. Marjoram is also good for the nerves and warms the stomach from the inside—an ideal herb for use in winter.

Nasturtiums

Nasturtiums came originally from Peru and Ecuador and were brought to Europe by the Spanish in the 16th century. However, it is not known whether they arrived at the same time as potatoes. The leaves and brightly-colored flowers can be used for decoration or chopped finely and mixed into salads or quark.

Pansy flowers

Pansies grow in gardens and along the roadside. They look pretty but they do not taste of anything. This makes them particularly good for decorating salads or the edges of gratin dishes, as they do not dominate or distort the flavor of the food itself.

A small sprig of lavender flowers gives mash a delicate tint and calms the nerves. Many herbs not only taste delicious but are also healthy and make food easier to digest.

Parsley

Parsley is to some extent a standard in the kitchen, although its use did not become widespread until the 16th century. Because of its high vitamin C content, parsley is considered to be very good for the health, but only if it is freshly chopped and sprinkled on food. It has an intense flavor, so should not be sprinkled too generously on potatoes.

Pepper

Pepper and salt are the two basic seasonings found on every restaurant table. What is usually on the table is black pepper. Green and black pepper are made from the unripe fruits, while white and red pepper come from the ripe fruits. If you want to go to where pepper grows, you will have to travel to India, Malaysia, Vietnam, Indonesia, or Brazil.

Rosemary

Rosemary, whose name comes from the Latin *ros marinus* "dew of the sea," grows in almost all countries in the Mediterranean region. It particularly likes sunny rocky slopes which catch the dew or spray from the sea. This slightly bitter tasting herb is especially popular in Mediterranean cuisine. Placing a small sprig of rosemary on top of potatoes baked in the oven gives them a delicate hint of flavor.

Thyme

Like rosemary, thyme comes originally from the countries around the shores of the Mediterranean. It can be cooked, for instance in stews, and makes heavy dishes easier to digest. If you prefer to work with a mixture of herbs, you will certainly have come across it in "Herbes de Provence."

Watercress

Watercress grows wild almost everywhere in Europe and parts of the United States and Asia, especially around springs of clear, pure water. Seek it out at farmers' markets and specialty stores. It is a member of the crucifer or brassica family, and can be cut almost all year round. The spicy, slightly bitter-tasting leaves can be mixed into salads along with the stems. It can also be combined with quark and herb butter. Herb quark with watercress goes particularly well with potatoes boiled in their skins.

Potato and herb salad with smoked salmon

Serves 4
2¼ lb (1 kg) small potatoes, waxy variety
1 bunch parsley
1 bunch mint
juice of 2 lemons
¼ tsp sugar
4 tbsp olive oil
9 oz (250 g) smoked salmon
salt, pepper

The mint brings a touch of freshness to this salad, which can also be served as a starter.

Wash the potatoes and put in a pan with just enough water to cover and boil with the lid on for about 25 minutes until tender but still firm. Rinse the parsley and mint under running water, pat dry. Pick off the leaves and chop roughly. In a salad bowl mix together the lemon juice, sugar, salt, and pepper until the salt and sugar have dissolved. Then beat in the olive oil with a hand whisk to give a creamy dressing.

Peel the potatoes, cut in quarters lengthways, and mix with the dressing. Leave for 10 minutes to let the flavors develop. Cut the salmon in strips and fold the salmon and herbs into the potatoes.

Tip

Black salsify rösti go well with this. Trim 8 black salsify sticks, peel, and grate. Mix with 1 tablespoon flour and 1 egg, and season with salt and pepper. Fry in a skillet with a little oil.

Asian potato and beef salad

Serves 4
generous 1 lb (500 g) purple potatoes, waxy variety
1 small cucumber
3 scallions
4 tbsp toasted sesame oil
4 tbsp lemon juice
2 fillet steaks (each about 7 oz/200 g)
2 tbsp sunflower oil
2 tbsp soy sauce
1 garlic clove
¼ tsp cayenne pepper
salt, pepper

Wash the potatoes and boil in just enough water to cover for about 30 minutes, or until tender but still firm, then peel and slice. Wash the cucumber, slice thinly, and arrange with the potatoes in a fan shape on a flat plate. Wash the scallions and cut diagonally in narrow rings. Mix together thoroughly 2 tablespoons of the sesame oil, 2 tablespoons of the lemon juice, salt, and pepper to taste, and pour over the scallions. Leave to let the flavors develop.

Heat the sunflower oil in a pan and fry the steaks on both sides for about 6 to 8 minutes, so they are still pink inside. In a small bowl, mix the remaining sesame oil with the soy sauce and the remaining lemon juice. Peel the garlic, crush in a garlic press or with the flat blade of a knife, add to the bowl, and season with salt, pepper, and cayenne pepper. Allow the meat to cool a little, then cut diagonally in thin slices and arrange on the cucumber. Drain the scallions, sprinkle over the salad and drizzle with the dressing.

Potato salad with apples, cheese, and walnuts

Serves 4—6
1¾ lb (800 g) small potatoes, waxy variety
2 red onions
1 small jar cornichons
2 fairly sharp apples, e.g. Granny Smith
a little lemon juice
½ cup (50 g) chopped walnuts
5½ oz (150 g) Emmental cheese
1 bunch chives
⅔ cup (150 g) natural yogurt
3 tbsp each vinegar and olive oil
2 tsp medium hot mustard
salt, black pepper

Wash the potatoes, put in a pan with just enough salted water to cover and cook with the lid on for about 25 to 30 minutes, or until tender but still firm. Peel the onions and chop finely. Drain and slice the cornichons. Peel the apples, cut into eight and remove the cores. Slice the apple segments thinly and drizzle immediately with lemon juice to prevent them from turning brown. Transfer all these ingredients to a bowl. Add the chopped walnuts.

Cut off the rind and dice the cheese. Rinse the chives under running water, pat dry, cut in rings, and add half to the cheese. Drain the potatoes, peel, allow to cool, and dice. Add to the other ingredients in the bowl. Using a hand whisk, beat the yogurt, vinegar, olive oil, mustard, with salt and pepper to taste, into a creamy dressing. Pour over the salad and mix. Sprinkle with the remaining chives.

Potato and asparagus salad with Kassler

Serves 4—6
1¾ lb (800 g) potatoes, waxy variety
1 tsp cumin seeds
1 bunch green asparagus
9 oz (250 g) piece boneless Kassler (or salted smoked pork)
1 bunch chives
5 tbsp white wine vinegar
1 tsp medium hot mustard
6 tbsp sunflower oil
salt, pepper

Wash the potatoes, put in a pan with the cumin seeds and just enough water to cover, and boil for about 30 minutes, or until tender but still firm. Wash the asparagus, peel the bottom third, and cut off the ends. Cut the asparagus spears in pieces ½ inch (1 cm) long. Cook in boiling salted water for 2 to 3 minutes, remove from the pan (reserving a scant ½ cup of the hot cooking liquid), rinse in ice cold water and drain well.

Cut the Kassler in small cubes. Wash the chives, pat dry, and cut in rounds. In a small bowl, beat together the white wine vinegar, mustard, oil, and salt and pepper to taste, with a hand blender until creamy. Mix in the chives.

Peel and slice the potatoes (not too thinly), transfer to a large bowl, and allow to cool a little. Pour over the reserved hot liquid from the asparagus pan and the dressing. Add the asparagus and the Kassler, mix, cover, and leave for 10 minutes to let the flavors develop, then season again to taste.

Green salad with asparagus, potatoes, spinach, peas, and fava beans

Wash the potatoes, put in a pan and boil in salted water for about 25 minutes or until tender but still firm.

Meanwhile peel the bottom third of the asparagus spears, cut off the woody ends, cut the spears in two, and cook al dente in boiling salted water for about 10 minutes. Drain, rinse in cold water, and leave to drain thoroughly. Blanch the beans in boiling water with a pinch of salt for about 8 minutes, adding the peas after 4 minutes, and cooking both together. Drain, rinse in cold water, and leave to drain. Wash the spinach, pick off the leaves, trim, and dry in a salad spinner.

Drain the potatoes, leave to cool until lukewarm, and slice. Mix with the remaining salad ingredients. Make a vinaigrette with the vinegar, mustard, and oil, and season with salt and pepper to taste. Drizzle over the salad and serve.

SERVES 4

14 oz (400 g) small potatoes, waxy variety
14 oz (400 g) green asparagus
5½ oz (150 g) fava (broad) beans
5½ oz (150 g) fresh peas
1 handful fresh young leaf spinach
2 tbsp white wine vinegar
½ tsp hot mustard
4 tbsp olive oil
salt, pepper

With the necessary know-how, any backyard, balcony, or patio can be made into a miniature potato field. The illustration (right) shows how the layers of potatoes gradually build up in the container.

Grow your own

Do you like potatoes, want to pick good ones, want to grow your own, but don't have a garden? What's the problem? Even a small balcony gives you enough space to enjoy the fun of harvesting your own potatoes. If you plant them in the spring in a tub, a bucket, or a growing bag specially produced for the purpose, you will be able to harvest the first of them in early summer.

You will need:
A balcony or patio or any other small, open-air space. A warm, sunny spot would be ideal.
Your chosen variety or varieties of potato. Your local garden equipment supplier will be able to offer advice on suitable varieties.
Tip: To be on the safe side, buy organic potatoes, to be sure they have not been treated with sprout inhibitors.
A suitable container. This could be a large flower pot, a plastic bucket, a wooden box, a burlap sack, a grow bag, or even a trash bag, depending on the space you have available and how many potatoes you want to grow.

Gravel or ceramic pellets for the drainage layer.

A 50/50 mix of topsoil and compost. You may be able to buy a prepared mix from your local garden equipment supplier. The amount needed will depend on the size of your chosen container.

What to do next:
First fill your container with a drainage layer of gravel or ceramic pellets about three fingers deep. If you are using plastic sacks, you will need to cut one or two holes in the base to allow water to run out freely.
Tip: You will also need to cut holes in a grow bag because, though these are filled with prepared growing compost, they do not have a drainage layer and can easily become waterlogged.
Then add a 6-inch (15-cm) layer of a mixture of soil and compost.
Tip: Mix in a handful of sand as well.
Place 3–5 seed potatoes on this first layer, depending on the size of the container. The potatoes should be about a finger length apart, i.e. around 3 inches (8 cm). Ideally the potatoes should have already begun to sprout when planted. This will give you an earlier harvest. If not, use your green fingers—in other words, be patient!
Tip: To bring forward sprouting, from the end of February leave your seed potatoes in a light place at 54–59 °F (12–15 °C) for about two weeks.

Spread more soil over the potatoes. If you are using a burlap sack or trash bag, roll down the top edge to a height of about 8 inches (20 cm) above the top of the soil, to allow as much light as possible to reach the plants while they are still small.

Leave the potatoes to sprout. As soon as the leaves have grown to about 4 – 5 inches (10 – 15 cm) in height, add enough soil to cover all but the green tips. This will cause several layers of new tubers to form, which will be ready for harvesting about 100 days after planting.
Take care not to let the soil dry out. Water the plants regularly, especially in hot, dry weather. Potato plants lose a lot of water through evaporation and the roots have only limited room in the container.
Tip: Do not water with ice cold water from the faucet. Even a firm potato can react badly to this kind of shock treatment, which makes it much more susceptible to disease. Rainwater is best.

Planting time: Early potato varieties can be planted as early as the end of March, medium early varieties not until the end of April. Potatoes are susceptible to frost damage and can be threatened by late spring frosts right up to mid-May. Cover the "potato patch" on frosty nights with protective fleece, foil, or coconut fiber so the leaves do not get frozen.

Harvesting time: After about 100 days. The potatoes are ripe when the leaves turn yellow and begin to wilt.

Italian potato salad

SERVES 4
1¾ lb (800 g) potatoes, waxy variety
1 sprig rosemary
generous 1 lb (500 g) beef tomatoes
3 tbsp red wine vinegar
2 tbsp balsamic vinegar
5 tbsp olive oil
1 medium onion
1 garlic clove
1 bunch basil
3 tbsp small capers
salt, pepper

Put the potatoes in a pan with the rosemary sprig, just cover with water, and boil with the lid on for about 30 minutes, or until tender but still firm. Scald the tomatoes, discard the peel, cut in half crossways, remove the seeds, and dice small.

In a large bowl mix together the red wine vinegar, balsamic vinegar, and olive oil with salt and pepper to taste, to make a creamy salad dressing. Peel the onion and the garlic clove, chop finely, and add to the bowl along with the chopped tomatoes.

Drain the potatoes, allow to cool a little, cut in ½ inch (1 cm) cubes, add to the bowl, and mix everything together. Wash the basil, pick off the leaves and mix in, together with the capers. Leave the salad briefly for the flavors to develop, then season to taste.

Potato and ham salad with grapes and cress

SERVES 4
11 oz (300 g) potatoes, waxy variety
10 seedless red grapes
4 oz (120 g) air-dried ham, sliced
2 tbsp white wine vinegar
1 tbsp lemon juice
5 tbsp olive oil
½ bunch small-leaf cress
capers (optional)
salt, pepper

Wash the potatoes and cook in boiling salted water for about 30 minutes, or until tender but still firm.

Meanwhile, wash the grapes and cut in half. Cut or tear the ham in small pieces. Mix together the vinegar, lemon juice, and oil, and season with salt and pepper to taste.

Drain the potatoes, rinse in cold water, peel, allow to cool, and dice small. Mix with the ham, grapes, capers, if using, and vinaigrette, season to taste, transfer to individual bowls or glasses and decorate with the cress.

Asian potato and carrot salad with sesame

Serves 4
1¾ lb (800 g) potatoes, waxy variety
generous 1 lb (500 g) carrots
5 tbsp sesame seeds
½ bunch cilantro
1 lemon
1 pinch sugar
3 tbsp soya oil
3 tbsp tahini (sesame paste)
salt, pepper

Wash the potatoes and boil in just enough water to cover them for about 25 minutes, or until tender but still firm. Peel the carrots and dice small. Boil in salted water for 3 minutes, tip into a strainer, rinse in ice cold water, and drain well.

Peel the potatoes and cut into ½ inch (1 cm) cubes. Transfer to a bowl, along with the diced carrots. Toast the sesame seeds in a dry pan until golden brown, leave to cool a little, and add to the bowl. Wash the cilantro, pick off the leaves, and chop roughly. Make a dressing of lemon juice, sugar, soya oil, tahini, salt, and pepper to taste. Pour over the other ingredients and mix in. Finally, fold the cilantro into the salad.

Variation: Asian meatballs and potato salad

Serves 4
1½ lb (700 g) potatoes, waxy variety
1 stale bread roll, crust removed
2 garlic cloves
2¼ cups (600 g) ground meat, preferably lamb
1 egg
1 tsp grated lemon rind
4 tbsp freshly chopped parsley
olive oil
1 red onion
juice of 1 untreated lemon
sumac
salt, pepper

Wash the potatoes and boil in salted water for 20—25 minutes, or until tender but still firm. Moisten the bread in lukewarm water and squeeze out as much of the moisture as you can. Peel the garlic and chop small. Add to the ground meat and knead together with the egg, grated lemon rind, bread, and 2 tablespoons of the freshly chopped parsley. Season with salt and pepper. Form into small, oval meatballs and fry in oil in a hot skillet until golden brown all round. Reduce the heat and allow the meatballs to cook through.

Peel the onion, cut in half and slice in narrow rings. Drain the potatoes, rinse in cold water, peel, and leave to cool. Dice, mix with the onions, the remaining parsley, lemon juice, and 4 tablespoons olive oil. Flavor to taste with salt and sumac.

Ensalada rusa — Russian salad

Serves 6
1½ lb (750 g) potatoes, predominantly waxy variety
¾ cup (150 g) green beans
2 medium (150 g) carrots
1¼ cups (150 g) frozen peas
3 egg yolks
2 tbsp lemon juice
1 cup (¼ liter) olive oil
salt, pepper

Although it is called Russian salad, this one is a Spanish specialty.

Wash the potatoes, put in a pan with just enough water to cover and boil with the lid on for about 30 minutes, or until tender but still firm. Allow to cool, peel, cut in ¾ inch (2 cm) cubes and transfer to a large bowl.
Trim the beans, wash, and cook in salted water for 10 minutes. Rinse in ice cold water and leave to drain. Peel the carrots, dice small, and cook for 3 minutes. Rinse in ice cold water and drain well. Heat the peas in boiling salted water for 1 minute, rinse in cold water and leave to drain. Add the vegetables to the potatoes in the bowl. Beat the egg yolks with a little salt, pepper, and lemon juice. Add the olive oil in a thin stream, beating vigorously all the time with a hand whisk or hand blender, to give a creamy mayonnaise. Add the mayonnaise to the bowl and mix gently with the other ingredients. Refrigerate for at least 20 minutes to allow the salad flavors to develop. Season again to taste before serving.

Potato salad with goat's cheese and grapes

Wash the potatoes thoroughly and boil in salted water for about 25 minutes until tender but still firm. Drain and leave to cool. Peel the onion and slice into rings. Wash the grapes, pat dry, and cut in half. Cut the potatoes in bite-size cubes and mix in a bowl with the grapes and onion rings.

Mix together the vinegar, sunflower oil, salt, pepper, and add to the prepared salad ingredients. Mix everything together and check the seasoning. Arrange the salad on plates and serve sprinkled with crumbled goat's cheese and finely chopped basil.

Serves 4

1¾ lb (800 g) early potatoes, waxy variety,
1 red onion
9 oz (250 g) seedless red grapes
4 tbsp white wine vinegar
8 tbsp sunflower oil
2 tbsp finely chopped basil leaves
9 oz (250 g) goat's cheese (roll)
salt, pepper

Potato salad with onions and cornichons

Serves 4
1¾ lb (800 g) potatoes, waxy variety
3½ oz (100 g) cornichons
1 red onion
2 tbsp olive oil
2 – 3 tbsp white wine vinegar
4 tbsp vegetable stock
salt, pepper
½ bunch parsley, chopped

Wash the potatoes thoroughly and cook in boiling salted water for about 25 minutes until tender but still firm. Tip into a sieve, drain, and leave to cool.

Slice or dice the cornichons. Peel the onion and chop finely. Cut the potatoes in bite-size cubes.

Heat the olive oil in a pan and fry the potato cubes until golden. Add the onion, sweat briefly with the potatoes, then mix in the cornichons, and tip everything into a bowl. Mix the vinegar and stock into the salad, season to taste with salt and pepper, and gently fold in the parsley. Season again and serve in individual bowls.

Potatoes in their skins with sheep's cheese

Wash the potatoes thoroughly and cook in boiling salted water for 25–30 minutes, or until tender but still firm. Rinse the oregano under running water, pat dry with paper towels, and pick off the leaves.

Drain the potatoes, let the steam evaporate, cut in quarters and arrange on plates. Season lightly with salt and pepper, crumble the Feta over them, and drizzle with olive oil. Sprinkle with oregano and serve.

SERVES 4

1¾ lb (800 g) potatoes, waxy variety

3 sprigs oregano

9 oz (250 g) Feta (preferably Greek origin Feta)

olive oil

salt, white pepper

Simple but Effective: Basic Recipes

People who pursue ever greater wealth, without ever allowing themselves time to enjoy it, are like hungry folk, who cook all the time but never sit down at table.

MARIE FREIFRAU VON EBNER-ESCHENBACH, 19TH-CENTURY DRAMATIST, NOVELIST, AND ESSAYIST

You need to know the basics

When it comes to cooking potatoes, there are a few classic recipes that constantly appear in different variations. If you have a good grasp of these basics, you can give free rein to your own imagination and experiment. If you have mastered classic mashed potato, you will have no problem introducing a hint of truffle, celery, or pumpkin. There is also a basic framework for dumplings, potato fritters, fried or roast potatoes, which you can then adapt to suit your own taste and the other components of the recipe.

Classic fried potatoes

Serves 4–6
1¾ lb (800 g) medium to large potatoes, waxy variety
4–6 tbsp sunflower oil
salt

Sadly, good fried potatoes are not so easy to find. In "Schumann's Bar" in Munich, roast beef with fried potatoes is a classic dish. Chef Charles Schumann will not delegate anyone else to prepare them.

Wash the potatoes, boil in a pan with just enough water to cover them for 45 to 60 minutes, or until tender but still firm. Pour off the water, peel the potatoes while still warm, which makes it easier, and allow to cool completely. They can also be boiled the previous day. Cut the potatoes in slices about ¼ inch (0.5 cm) thick. Heat the sunflower oil well in a large, preferably non-stick, skillet. Spread the potato slices out flat and fry on one side for about 5 minutes until golden brown. Turn the potatoes with a spatula and fry on the other side until golden brown. Drain on paper towels and sprinkle with salt to taste.

Tip
Only use fat that can be heated to a high temperature, such as dripping, clarified butter, or oil. Butter turns brown with heat and is therefore not suitable.

Country potatoes

Serves 4
2¼ lb (1 kg) potatoes, waxy variety
4–5 tbsp olive oil
1 tbsp honey
2 tbsp sweet ground paprika
¼ tsp chili powder
sea salt for sprinkling

Preheat the oven to 425 °F (220 °C). Wash the potatoes thoroughly, pat dry, and cut each into eight segments. In a bowl mix the oil, honey, paprika, and chili powder. Line a baking sheet with parchment. Turn the potatoes in the coating mixture and arrange on the baking sheet. Bake in the preheated oven for 30 minutes or until tender. Sprinkle with sea salt and serve.

French fries

Serves 4
2¼ lb (1 kg) potatoes, waxy variety
6 cups (1½ liters) vegetable oil, for frying
sea salt

Wash the potatoes, peel, and with a sharp knife, cut lengthways into sticks the thickness of a pencil. Heat the oil in a deep-fat fryer or a large pan. The perfect temperature has been reached when little bubbles form when you stick the handle of a wooden spoon into the oil. Fry the potato sticks in batches in the hot oil for about 3 to 4 minutes until golden yellow. Remove from the fat with a slotted spoon, drain briefly on paper towels, and season with sea salt.

Tip
The fries will be less greasy, if you blanch them briefly in boiling salted water before frying. Then leave them to drain thoroughly on paper towels and fry as described above. Taste first before adding salt to the finished fries.

Boiled potatoes

Serves 4
2¼ lb (1 kg) potatoes, predominantly waxy variety
salt
1 pinch cumin seeds
2–3 tbsp butter

Peel the potatoes, cut in halves or quarters depending on the size and put in a pan. Cover completely with water, add salt to taste, and sprinkle the cumin seeds into the water. Bring to a boil, then reduce the heat, cover, and boil for about 20 minutes, or until tender. Prod the potatoes with a fork. If it goes in easily, they are done. If not, boil for a little longer.
Drain the potatoes in a colander and return to the pan. Turn off the heat and put the pan back on the hotplate, without the lid, for a couple of minutes to allow the steam and remaining water to evaporate, shaking the pan occasionally. Transfer the potatoes to a warmed bowl and dot with flakes of butter.

Potato purée

Serves 4
1¾ lb (800 g) potatoes, floury variety
1 tsp cumin seeds (optional)
3½ tbsp (50 g) butter
½–¾ cup (150–200 ml) hot milk
1 pinch grated nutmeg
salt, pepper

This puréed form of mashed potato also lends itself to piping (potato rosettes, on a fish pie for example), but take care when adding the milk not to let the mash become too loose or it will not keep its shape when piped.
Wash the potatoes thoroughly, put in a pan, just cover with water, add the cumin, if using, and boil for about 25 minutes, or until soft when pierced with a fork. Peel the potatoes and mash through a potato ricer. Gradually mix in the butter and hot milk alternately, adjusting the latter to the texture of the mashed potato, and season to taste with salt, pepper, and nutmeg.

Potatoes boiled in their skins with guacamole

Wash the potatoes thoroughly, put in a pan, just cover with water and boil with the lid on for about 25 minutes, or until tender when pierced with a fork.

Meanwhile peel the onion and garlic and chop finely. Scrape the seeds out of the chile, wash, and cut into small pieces. Wash the cilantro, pat dry, pick off the leaves, and chop finely. Cut the avocados in half, pit, and scoop out the flesh into a bowl. Crush well with a fork, gradually mixing in the lemon juice. Mix in the onion, garlic, chile, and cilantro and season to taste with salt and pepper. Drain the potatoes and peel if desired, or mix them still in their skins with the guacamole.

SERVES 4

2¼ lb (1 kg) small, even-sized potatoes, waxy variety
1 medium onion
1 garlic clove
1 small, red chile
½ bunch cilantro
3 ripe avocados
juice of ½ lemon
salt, pepper

TIP

A dip mixed from herb quark and guacamole also goes really well with potatoes boiled in their skins.

Classic mashed potatoes

SERVES 4
1¾ lb (800 g) potatoes, floury variety
1 tsp cumin seeds (optional)
3½ tbsp (50 g) butter
salt, pepper
1 pinch grated nutmeg

Put the potatoes in a pan with the cumin, if using, just cover with water and boil for about 25 minutes until soft when pierced with a fork. Peel the potatoes and mash into a warmed bowl with a potato masher or ricer. Mix in the butter and season to taste with salt, pepper, and nutmeg.

Cold Variation: Potato spread

SERVES 6—8
mashed potato as described above
scant 1¼ cups (300 g) sour cream
1 onion
2 garlic cloves
1 bunch chives
1 bunch broad-leaved garlic
½ cup (50 g) grated Parmesan
3½ oz (100 g) smoked bacon
salt, pepper

A popular spread for bread from southern Germany and Austria.

Prepare the mashed potato as described above and leave to cool. Then mix in the sour cream and season to taste with salt and pepper. Peel the onion and garlic and chop finely. Wash the chives and broad-leaved garlic, pat dry with paper towels, and cut into small rolls or strips. Mix these and the Parmesan into the mash. Dice the smoked bacon and fry in a hot skillet. Allow to cool a little and mix into the mash.

TIP
If desired, apart from the sour cream, you need not include all the listed ingredients into the mash.

New York potato pancakes

SERVES 4
2¼ lb (1 kg) potatoes, waxy variety
1 medium onion
2 eggs
3 tbsp all-purpose flour
½ tsp baking powder
6 tbsp clarified butter for frying
salt, pepper

Peel the potatoes and grate coarsely into a bowl. Leave to stand for 30 to 40 minutes. They will release juice and oxidize. Peel the onion and grate coarsely. Cover and set aside. Tip the grated potatoes into a strainer and rinse under cold running water. Wrap in a clean dish towel and squeeze out as much moisture as you can, then transfer to a bowl. Press the onions gently to release excess moisture and add to the bowl. Mix in the eggs, flour, and baking powder. Season the mixture to taste with salt and pepper.
Heat the clarified butter in a large skillet. Add a large spoonful of the potato mixture and press flat. Fry on both sides until golden yellow, leave to drain on paper towels, then keep warm in the oven at 125 °F (50 °C). Continue until all the potato mixture has been used.

Traditional and International Oven Bakes

Friendship is the noblest feeling of which human hearts are capable.
Carl Hilty, 19th-century Swiss philosopher, writer, and lawyer

From the oven – gratins & others

Potatoes cooked in the oven, in the form of gratins or bakes, are perfect as both side dishes and main courses. On the Canary Islands, papas arrugadas – potatoes with a coating of sea salt – are the hot favorite. These "wrinkled potatoes" are served with Mojo Verde or Mojo Rosso. Served with steak or on their own, there is much more to potatoes than their nondescript appearance might suggest.

Gratin Dauphinoise – potato gratin

SERVES 4
1 garlic clove
fat for greasing
1¾ lb (800 g) potatoes, floury variety
1 pinch grated nutmeg
scant ½ cup (100 ml) milk
1 cup (250 ml) heavy cream
generous 1¼ cups (150 g) grated Gruyère
2 tbsp butter
salt, pepper

Peel the garlic clove, cut in half lengthwise, and rub the inside of a large ovenproof dish with the cut surface. Then grease the dish. Peel the potatoes, wash, and slice thinly. Arrange the potato slices in the dish, slightly overlapping and, if possible, in a single thick layer. Season with salt, pepper, and nutmeg.

Preheat the oven to 350 °F (180 °C). Beat together the milk, cream, and grated cheese and pour evenly over the potatoes. Top with flakes of butter. Bake on the middle shelf of the preheated oven for about 1 hour, until a nice crust has formed.

Baked potatoes with salmon

SERVES 4
4 large potatoes (each about 8 oz/220 g), waxy variety
1 tsp cumin seeds
4 salmon steaks (each about 8 oz/200 g)
2 tbsp lemon juice
1 bunch chives
½ bunch parsley
a few mint leaves
1 small garlic clove
1 cup (250 ml) crème fraîche
salt, pepper

Wash the potatoes thoroughly under running water and boil with the cumin in salted water in a pan with the lid on for 20 to 25 minutes, or until tender. Rinse the salmon in cold water, pat dry, drizzle with lemon juice, and season with salt and pepper. Preheat the oven to 480 °F (250 °C). Wash the chives and chop finely. Wash the parsley and mint under running water, pick off the leaves and chop finely. Peel the garlic and chop finely. Mix together the crème fraîche, herbs, and garlic, season with salt and pepper, cover, and refrigerate. Drain the potatoes, cut a cross in them, and wrap individually in aluminum foil. Arrange on a baking sheet and bake in the oven for about 20 minutes, depending on size. Ten minutes before the potatoes are ready, heat the oil in a skillet and fry the salmon for about 8 minutes, turning once. Remove the potatoes from the foil, top each with a blob of crème fraîche, and serve with the salmon.

Swordfish on a bed of potatoes

Serves 4
2¼ lb (1 kg) evenly sized potatoes, floury variety
4 swordfish steaks (each 7 oz/200 g)
1 bunch cilantro
6 tbsp olive oil
juice of 1 lemon
3 garlic cloves
¼ tsp cayenne pepper
salt, pepper

Wash the potatoes thoroughly under running water and put in a pan with just enough water to cover. Boil the potatoes with the lid on for about 30 minutes, or until soft. Rinse the swordfish steaks in cold water, pat dry, and arrange side by side on a dish. Wash the cilantro, pick off the leaves and chop roughly. In a small bowl, mix 4 tablespoons of the olive oil together with the lemon juice. Peel the garlic, crush in a press, or with the flat blade of a knife, and add to the bowl. Season the marinade with salt, pepper, and cayenne pepper and pour evenly over the fish. Cover and refrigerate for 20 minutes to let the flavors develop.

Preheat the oven to 390 °F (200 °C). Brush a gratin dish with the remaining olive oil. Drain the potatoes, peel, and cut in fairly thick slices. Spread over the bottom of the gratin dish and season with salt and pepper. Place the fish on top and drizzle with the remaining marinade. Cover the dish with aluminum foil or a lid and bake on the middle shelf of the preheated oven for 20 to 25 minutes, or until tender. Remove from the oven and serve in the gratin dish.

Papas arrugadas

Serves 4
8 potatoes (each about 3½ oz/100 g), floury variety
8¾ lb (4 kg) coarse sea salt
5 tbsp garlic cloves
⅔ cup (150 g) salted butter
1 bunch flat-leaf parsley
1 medium onion
3½ tbsp (50 ml) olive oil
salt, pepper

Preheat the oven to 300 °F (150 °C). Wash the potatoes thoroughly. Line a baking sheet with baking parchment and use half the sea salt to make mounds about 1½ inches (4 cm) high. Stand a potato on each mound, cover with the remaining sea salt and bake on the middle shelf of the preheated oven for 50 minutes, then leave to stand for 15 minutes.

Peel the garlic, chop finely, and mix with the butter. Season with salt and pepper and refrigerate. Wash the parsley and tear in pieces. Peel the onion, cut in quarters, and purée finely in a blender with the parsley and olive oil. Season with salt and pepper. Break open the salt crust, remove the potatoes and serve with the garlic butter and the parsley sauce.

To accompany: Mojo verde

1 bunch cilantro
1 bunch flat-leaf parsley
8 – 10 garlic cloves
1 red bell pepper
1 red chile, 1 tsp sea salt,
1 tsp cumin, 1 pinch sugar
1¼ cups (300 ml) olive oil
3½ tbsp (50 ml) white wine vinegar

Wash the cilantro and the parsley, shake dry, pick off the leaves. Peel the garlic and cut the cloves in half. Scrape the seeds and pith from the bell pepper and chile and cut in small pieces. Tip all of these into a deep bowl with the sea salt, cumin, and sugar. Mix with a hand blender, gradually adding in the olive oil and white wine vinegar, until a smooth paste is produced.

Beef, leek, and potato pie

For a 10-inch (26 cm)-diameter pie dish
11 oz (300 g) frozen puff pastry, thawed and ready to roll
1¼ lb (600 g) shoulder of beef
2 tbsp oil
1 tbsp flour
1½ cups (350 ml) meat stock
14 oz (400 g) leeks
1¼ lb (500 g) potatoes, predominantly waxy variety
1 egg yolk
1 tbsp milk
salt, pepper

The English specialty leek and potato pie is a popular vegetarian dish, but it can be enriched by the addition of chicken or ham. However, for this recipe, beef is the choice.

Cut the meat into ⅝ inch (1.5 cm) cubes. Heat the oil in a roasting pan and brown the diced meat on all sides. Season with salt and pepper, dust with the flour, and stir in. Pour over the meat stock, cover, and simmer over low heat for 30 minutes.
Wash and trim the leeks and cut in thin rings. Peel the potatoes, rinse, and cut into ⅓-inch (1 cm) cubes. Add the leeks and potatoes to the meat and cook together for 10 minutes. Season with salt and pepper, remove from the heat and allow to cool.
Preheat the oven to 440 °F (225 °C). Roll out the pastry to a round sheet slightly larger than the pie dish. Tip the meat and vegetable mixture into the pie dish, place the sheet of pastry lightly on top, slightly overlapping the edge of the dish. Press the pastry firmly around the edge of the dish. Slash a cross in the centre to allow the steam to escape. Beat together the egg yolk and milk and brush over the pastry. Bake the pie on the middle shelf of the preheated oven for 15 minutes.

Herb and garlic potatoes

Serves 4
scant ½ cup (100 ml) olive oil
2¼ lb (1 kg) small, evenly sized potatoes, waxy variety
5 garlic cloves
1 sprig each of thyme, oregano and rosemary
salt, pepper

This can be served as a delicious accompaniment to broiled meat, fried fish, or also with a large salad to make a vegetarian meal.

Preheat the oven to 400 °F (200 °C). Line a baking sheet with aluminum foil and brush with 3 tablespoons of the olive oil. Wash the potatoes thoroughly and rub dry. Cut in quarters and tip into a bowl. Season well with salt and pepper.
Wash the herbs under running water, then pick off the leaves and chop finely. Peel the garlic and chop finely. Add to the potatoes, along with the herbs and the remaining olive oil and mix together thoroughly.
Spread the potatoes over the baking sheet and bake on the middle shelf of the oven for 30 minutes until golden brown.

Ofenguck (Peek-in-the-Oven Casserole)

SERVES 4
2¼ lb (1 kg) potatoes, floury variety
3½ oz (100 g) cooked ham
3 oz (80 g) smoked bacon
3½ oz (100 g) Emmental
1 cup (250 ml) light cream, or milk
1 pinch grated nutmeg
fat for greasing
4 eggs
3 tbsp grated Sbrinz or Emmental
½ bunch chives
salt, pepper

Peel the potatoes, cut into quarters, and boil in salted water for about 20 minutes or until soft. Meanwhile, cut the rind off the ham, bacon, and Emmental and cut in small cubes.

Preheat the oven to 400 °F (200 °C). Press the hot potatoes through a ricer. Mix with the cream, diced ham, and cheese and season with salt, pepper, and nutmeg.

Grease an ovenproof dish, tip in the mixture and make eight depressions in it. Break an egg into each of four of these depressions and fill the other four with diced bacon. Sprinkle the top with grated cheese and bake on the middle shelf of the oven for 25 to 30 minutes, until the eggs have set hard. Wash the chives, snip into small pieces and sprinkle over the top.

Potato lasagna with beet sauce

Peel the garlic clove, cut in half lengthwise and rub the inside of a large gratin dish with the cut surface. Then grease the dish with 1 tablespoon of the butter. Preheat the oven to 350 °F (180 °C).
Peel the potatoes, and slice very thinly. Line base of the dish with a layer of potatoes and season with salt, pepper, and nutmeg. Cover with a layer of cheese. Continue in this way until all the potatoes and cheese have been used, finishing with a layer of potatoes.
Beat the milk and eggs together and pour evenly over the potatoes. Top with flakes of the remaining butter. Bake the potato lasagna for about 1 hour, until a nice crust has formed.
Meanwhile, coarsely dice the beet and simmer for 10 minutes with the vegetable stock and crème fraîche. Purée finely with a hand blender and season to taste with salt and pepper. Serve the potato lasagna with the beet sauce.

SERVES 4
1 garlic clove
2 tbsp butter
1¾ lb (800 g) potatoes, floury variety
1 pinch grated nutmeg
5½ oz (150 g) cheese from unpasteurized milk, e.g. Comté, thinly sliced
1¼ cups (300 ml) milk
2 eggs
1 cup (250 g) cooked beet
scant ½ cup (100 ml) vegetable stock
6 tbsp (100 g) crème fraîche
salt, pepper

Mallorcan Tumbet

SERVES 4
generous 1 lb (500 g) red bell peppers
1¾ lb (800 g) beef tomatoes
5½ oz (150 g) onions
3 garlic cloves
6 tbsp olive oil
2 bay leaves
1 pinch cinnamon
1¾ lb (800 g) potatoes, floury variety
1 cup (250 ml) vegetable stock
2 small eggplant (approx. 1¼ lb/600 g)
flour for tossing
salt, pepper

When I was on Mallorca many years ago, I ate this almost every day, because it tastes just wonderful. Unfortunately, it takes some time to prepare.

Preheat the oven to 390 °F (200 °C). Cut the bell peppers in half lengthwise and scrape out the seeds and pith. Wash them, arrange cut-side down on the broiler rack, and roast for about 20 minutes. Remove from the oven and allow to cool a little. Then remove the skins and cut in wide strips. Scald the beef tomatoes, discard the skins and seeds, and chop roughly.

Peel the onions and garlic and chop finely. Fry until transparent in a large skillet with 2 tablespoons of the olive oil. Add the tomatoes and the bay leaves, season with salt, pepper, and cinnamon, and cook for 10 minutes over low heat.

Peel the potatoes and slice thinly. Cook for about 10 minutes in a large skillet with the vegetable stock. Wash and trim the eggplant, and cut into slices about ¼ inch (0.5 cm) thick. Fry in a skillet in the remaining olive oil. Grease the inside of a large gratin dish, fill with alternating layers of potatoes, eggplant, and strips of bell pepper, seasoning with salt and pepper as you go. Pour over the tomato sauce and cook on the middle shelf of the preheated oven for 30 minutes.

Potato bake with ham

SERVES 4
2¼ lb (1 kg) potatoes, floury variety
1 tsp cumin seeds
7 oz (200 g) onions
2 tbsp butter
1 tsp each of thyme and oregano
7 oz (200 g) cooked ham, sliced
3 eggs
generous 1½ cups (375 ml) milk
9 oz (250 g) raclette cheese, sliced
1 pinch nutmeg
fat for greasing
salt, pepper

Wash the potatoes, and put in a pan with just enough water to cover. Add the cumin, and boil with the lid on for about 25 minutes, or until soft. Meanwhile, peel the onions and cut into thin rings.

Heat the butter in a skillet and fry the onion rings lightly until transparent. Season with salt, pepper, thyme, and oregano. Remove the pan from the heat. Cut the ham in small pieces.

Beat the eggs and milk together and season with salt, pepper, and nutmeg. Preheat the oven to 425 °F (220 °C). Grease a gratin dish. Peel and slice the potatoes. Then fill the dish with alternate layers of slightly overlapping potato and cheese slices, spreading fried onion rings and ham pieces in between. Pour the beaten egg and milk evenly over the top and bake on the middle shelf of the preheated oven for about 30 minutes. If the surface browns too quickly, cover with aluminum foil.

Potato and sauerkraut bake with bratwurst

Wash the potatoes, put in a pan with just enough water to cover and boil with the lid on for about 25 minutes, or until soft. Peel the onion, chop finely, and fry lightly in 1 tablespoon of the butter in a wide sauté pan until transparent. Add the sauerkraut, fry lightly with the onion, and pour over the apple juice. Season to taste with salt and pepper, cover, and cook for 15 minutes over medium heat. Drain the potatoes, peel, and mash in a large bowl with 1 tablespoon of the butter.

Preheat the oven to 350 °F (180 °C). Grease a gratin dish. Fry the sausages briefly in half the remaining butter and cut in slices. Mix the sausages, sauerkraut mixture, sour cream, and mustard in with the potatoes and season (again) with salt and pepper. Transfer the mixture to the gratin dish and smooth over the surface. Sprinkle with breadcrumbs and top with flakes of the remaining butter. Bake on the middle shelf of the oven for about 30 minutes.

Serves 4

1¼ lb (600 g) potatoes, floury variety

1 onion

4 tbsp butter

generous 1 lb (500 g) sauerkraut

scant ½ cup (100 ml) apple juice

8 bratwurst or similar sausages

generous ¾ cup (200 g) sour cream

2 tsp wholegrain mustard

4 tbsp breadcrumbs

fat for greasing

salt, pepper

Zucchini and potato gratin

A satisfying accompaniment for meat, fish, and vegetables, or a vegetarian main dish for two people.

Peel the onion and garlic, chop finely and fry lightly in 1 tablespoon of the butter, mixing in the thyme. Preheat the oven to 400 °F (200 °C). Peel the potatoes, wash, and slice thinly. Wash the zucchini, remove the stalk ends, and cut in slightly thicker slices than the potatoes.

Grease an ovenproof dish. Arrange the slices of potatoes and zucchini so they slightly overlap, spreading the onion mixture in between. Season with salt, pepper, and nutmeg. Mix the cream and grated cheese together, pour over the other ingredients, and bake on the middle shelf of the oven for 50 minutes.

Serves 4

1 large onion

2 garlic cloves

2 tbsp butter

1 tbsp fresh thyme

1¾ lb (800 g) potatoes, floury variety

generous 1 lb (500 g) zucchini

grated nutmeg

1 cup (250 g) heavy cream

scant 1 cup (100 g) grated Appenzeller, or other hard cheese

salt, pepper

Potato and asparagus bake

SERVES 4
2¼ lb (1 kg) potatoes, floury variety
generous 1 lb (500 g) green asparagus
1 large onion
2 tbsp butter
1 bunch chives
3 eggs
¾ cup (200 g) cream cheese with herbs
grated nutmeg
ground paprika
salt, pepper

Wash the potatoes and put in a pan with just enough water to cover. Boil with the lid on for 30 minutes, or until soft. Wash the asparagus, peel the bottom third and cut off the ends. Cut the asparagus spears diagonally in ½-inch (1 cm)-long pieces and blanch in boiling salted water for 5 minutes. Rinse in ice cold water and drain thoroughly. Meanwhile, peel the onion and chop finely. Heat 1 tablespoon of the butter in a skillet and fry the onion lightly until soft. Wash the chives and cut into thin rings. Peel the potatoes and press through a ricer. Mix the eggs, cream cheese, chives, and fried onions into the mashed potato and season well with salt, pepper, paprika, and nutmeg. Fold in the asparagus.
Preheat the oven to 350 °F (180 °C). Grease an ovenproof dish with the remaining butter. Transfer the potato and asparagus mixture to the dish. Bake on the middle shelf of the preheated oven for 45 minutes.

Potato soufflé with ricotta and Parmesan

SERVES 4
2¼ lb (1 kg) potatoes, predominantly waxy variety
1 medium onion
2 garlic cloves
1 tbsp butter
1 bunch parsley
9 oz (250 g) ricotta or low-fat quark
scant ½ cup (50 g) grated Parmesan
3 eggs
grated nutmeg
fat for greasing
salt, pepper

Wash the potatoes, put in a pan with just enough water to cover, and boil with the lid on for about 30 minutes, or until tender.
Meanwhile peel the onion and garlic and chop finely. Melt the butter in a skillet and fry the chopped onion over low heat until transparent. Wash the parsley, pull off the leaves and chop finely. Add to the skillet and fry briefly with the onion. Remove from the heat and allow to cool.
Preheat the oven to 400 °F (200 °C). Drain the potatoes, peel, allow the steam to evaporate, and press into a bowl through a ricer. Mix the onions, ricotta, and Parmesan into the potatoes.
Separate the eggs. Mix the yolks into the potato mixture and season to taste with salt, pepper, and nutmeg. Beat the egg whites into peaks and fold evenly into the mixture. Grease a soufflé dish (capacity 1½ quarts/1.5 liters) and spoon the potato mixture into it. Bake on the bottom shelf of the oven for 45 to 50 minutes. Remove from the oven and serve immediately. Do not open the oven during cooking, otherwise the soufflé will collapse.

Sissy Sonnleitner

Together with her husband and now with her daughter as well, Sissy Sonnleitner has been running the Landhaus Kellerwand hotel in Kötschach-Mauthen (Austria) for over 30 years. She has won many awards for her regional cuisine—influenced by the cuisine of the Alps-Adriatic area—including a Michelin star in 2001 and 3 Gault Millau toques in 2008.

Kärntner Nudeln (Austrian filled dough pockets)

For the dough
1⅔ cups (250 g) coarse wheat
½ cup (120 ml) water

For the filling
1 small leek
11 oz (300 g) potatoes, floury variety
2 tbsp chopped onions
7 tbsp (100 g) butter
1½ cups (250 g) Bröseltopfen quark, or cottage cheese drained for 2 hours
2 tbsp breadcrumbs
1 tbsp sour cream
chopped chervil
clarified butter

Knead the flour and water to a firm dough and leave to rest for about 30 minutes. Cut the leek into thin strips.
Peel the potatoes, boil in salted water until soft and then press through a ricer. Fry the onions and leek lightly in butter until golden yellow and mix into the potato, along with the remaining ingredients, except the clarified butter. Leave for 30 minutes for the flavors to develop.
Roll out the dough to a thickness of ⅛ inch (3 mm) and cut out circles about 3 inches (8 cm) in diameter, place about 1½ oz (40 g) filling on each and fold over the dough. Seal the edges firmly with the tines of a fork. Drop them into boiling salted water, stirring regularly so they do not stick to the bottom of the pan. When they float to the surface, boil for about 2 minutes more and then scoop them out with a slotted spoon. Drain well and serve with the clarified butter.

Tip
It is important for the flavor of the nudeln that the onions should be fried until golden yellow.

Oven-baked potatoes with a caper and olive vinaigrette

Serves 4
4 large potatoes, floury variety
¾ cup (100 g) black olives, pitted
3 tbsp (40 g) capers
4 sun-dried tomatoes in oil
lemon juice, 4 tbsp olive oil
4 tbsp chicken soup or fish stock

Preheat the oven to 400 °F (200 °C). Wash the potatoes, pierce with a thin skewer and wrap in aluminum foil. Bake for 45—60 minutes in the preheated oven. Meanwhile, drain the olives and capers and chop the olives small. Wash the tomatoes and chop small. Make the dressing by mixing the olives, capers, and tomatoes together with the lemon juice, olive oil, and chicken soup or fish stock.
Serve the potatoes hot from the oven with the vinaigrette.

Moussaka

SERVES 6
2 small eggplant
olive oil, for cooking
generous 1 lb (500 g) beef tomatoes
1 onion
2 garlic cloves
2½ cups (600 g) mixed ground meat
1 tsp dried rosemary
1 tsp dried thyme
1 bay leaf
½ cup (175 ml) stock
1¼ lb (600 g) potatoes, floury variety
scant 1 cup (100 g) grated hard goat's cheese, or Parmesan
salt, pepper

FOR THE BÉCHAMEL SAUCE
2 cups (500 ml) milk
3½ tbsp (50 g) butter
⅓ cup (50 g) all-purpose flour
salt, pepper
1 pinch grated nutmeg

Trim the eggplant, wash, and slice thinly. Brown in a large skillet in 4 tablespoons olive oil. Season with salt and pepper and set aside. Scald the tomatoes, peel, remove the seeds, and cut into small pieces. Peel the onions and garlic, chop finely, and brown lightly in 2 tablespoons olive oil. Mix in the ground meat and fry until crumbly. Add the tomatoes, rosemary, thyme, and bay leaf, and pour over the stock. Fry gently over low heat for 10 minutes without a lid. Remove the bay leaf.

To make the Béchamel sauce, bring the milk to a boil. Melt the butter in a pan. Add the flour and brown lightly. Stir in the hot milk with a hand whisk and simmer the sauce over low heat for about 10 minutes, stirring continuously, until it thickens. Season with salt, pepper, and nutmeg.

Peel the potatoes and slice thinly. Preheat the oven to 350 °F (180 °C). Brush a large ovenproof dish with olive oil and line the base with potatoes. Cover with a layer of ground meat and then a layer of eggplant. Continue in the same way until all the ingredients have been used. Sprinkle with the cheese. Lastly, pour over the Béchamel sauce and bake on the middle shelf of the oven for 1 hour.

Ground beef and potato bake

SERVES 4–6
1¾ lb (800 g) potatoes, floury variety
7 tbsp (100 g) butter
⅔ cup (150 ml) milk
2 onions
olive oil, for cooking
3½ cups (750 g) ground beef
9 oz (250 g) tomatoes
6 tbsp (50 g) raisins
1 pinch ground cumin
6 tbsp (50 g) pine nuts
1 bunch parsley
salt, pepper

Peel the potatoes, dice roughly, and boil in a little water with the lid on for about 20 minutes, or until soft. Then press through a ricer, mix in the butter and milk, and season with salt and pepper.

Peel the onions, chop finely, and fry lightly in a large skillet with 3 tablespoons olive oil. Add the ground meat and fry until crumbly. Meanwhile, scald the tomatoes, peel, remove the seeds, chop roughly and add to the pan along with the raisins. Season with salt, pepper, and cumin and set aside. Preheat the oven to 350 °F (180 °C). Toast the pine nuts in a dry, non-stick skillet until golden brown. Wash the parsley, tear off the leaves and chop finely. Mix the pine nuts and parsley into the ground meat.

Brush an ovenproof dish with olive oil. Spoon in half the mashed potato, and spread the ground meat over it. Top with the remaining mashed potato and smooth over. Bake in the preheated oven for 30 minutes.

Potatoes filled with broccoli and cheese

Serves 4
generous 1 lb (500 g) broccoli
8 even-sized potatoes (each about 7 oz/200 g), waxy variety
7 oz (200 g) Roquefort
3 tbsp crème fraîche
grated nutmeg
fat for greasing
salt, pepper

Trim the broccoli, wash, and cut into very small florets. Peel the stems and cut into rings. Blanch in boiling salted water for 2 minutes, tip into a colander, drain well, and allow to cool. Scrub the potatoes under cold running water, dry, and cut in half lengthwise. Using a small knife or a teaspoon with a sharp edge, hollow them out, leaving an edge of about ⅓ inch (1 cm). Preheat the oven to 325 °F (160 °C). Dice the scooped-out potato flesh very small and put into a bowl with the broccoli. Crumble the cheese and add to the bowl. Stir in the crème fraîche and season the mixture well with salt, pepper, and nutmeg. Fill the hollowed-out potato halves with the mixture. Grease an ovenproof dish and place the potatoes in it side by side. Spread the remaining filling between the potatoes and bake on the middle shelf of the preheated oven for about 45 minutes.

Classic German baked potatoes

Serves 4
4 large potatoes (each about 7½ oz/220 g), floury variety
1 tsp cumin seeds
3 tbsp lemon juice
2 bunch chives
generous ¾ cup (200 g) sour cream
salt, pepper

Wash the potatoes, put them in a pan and just cover with water. Add a pinch of salt and the cumin and boil with the lid on for 25 minutes, or until soft.

Preheat the oven to 425 °F (220 °C). Wash the chives and chop into small rings. Mix the sour cream with the lemon juice, season with salt and pepper, mix in the chives, and refrigerate.

Remove the potatoes from the pan, pat dry, cut a deep cross in the top, press a little, and wrap individually in aluminum foil. Place them directly on the oven shelf and bake for 15 to 20 minutes, depending on size.

Remove the potatoes from the foil and pour over the sour cream.

Mashed potato gratin on a bed of artichokes

Boil the potatoes in just enough water to cover, with the lid on, for about 30 minutes. Remove the leaves and the inner fibers, the "hair," from the artichokes and immediately brush the artichoke bases all over with lemon juice. Put them in a pan with boiling salted water and cook for 15 minutes over medium heat. Remove from the pan, drain, and transfer to a greased gratin dish. Preheat the oven to 350 °F (180 °C). Peel the potatoes and press through a ricer. Mix in the butter and enough milk to give a thick, creamy purée. Season with salt, pepper, and nutmeg, mix in the Parmesan, and spread over the artichoke bases. Bake on the middle shelf of the oven for about 10 minutes until golden brown .

SERVES 4
1¾ lb (800 g) potatoes, floury variety
8 large artichokes
juice of 2 lemons
3½ tbsp (50 ml) milk
3½ tbsp (50 g) butter
grated nutmeg
¼ cup (30 g) grated Parmesan
fat for greasing
salt, pepper

Anja Gottschall – Bavarian Potato Queen 2012

My home district of Neuburg-Schrobenhausen is the biggest contiguous potato-growing area in Bavaria. So I grew up with potatoes, in the truest sense of the word—perfect conditions for becoming a Bavarian potato Queen. I come from a farm with around 100 acres (40 hectares) of potato fields. My parents took me out to the fields with them when I was a child. That was where I first came across the "super tuber." Harvest is always a very special time for me and the period from the end of August to the beginning of October is an exceptionally busy time for us.

When it comes to lunch, I can say one thing for certain: on five days a week we have potatoes prepared in a wide variety of ways. My favorite dish is potatoes boiled in their skins and served with quark. If I have plenty of time, I also like to make the recipe below:

Potato tray bake

Serves 4

- 4½ lb (2 kg) potatoes, waxy variety
- herbs from the garden, e.g. parsley, chives, oregano, lovage
- 1¾ cups (400 g) heavy cream
- 1¾ cups (400 g) grated smoked Emmental, or other alpine cheese
- fat, for greasing
- herb salt, pepper

Preheat the oven to about 350 °F (180 °C). Wash the potatoes and boil in a pan filled with salted water for about 25 minutes, or until tender. Drain the potatoes, peel, and slice. Wash the herbs, shake dry, and chop. Mix the cream with the grated cheese.
Place a layer of potato slices in a greased gratin dish and sprinkle with some of the herbs. Cover with some of the cheese mixture. Repeat the layers until all the ingredients have been used. Season with herb salt and pepper and bake in the oven for 25 to 30 minutes.

Oven-baked potatoes with cheese

Wash the potatoes thoroughly and boil in salted water for 20 to 25 minutes until tender. Preheat the oven to 425 °F (220 °C). Wash the scallions, trim, and cut in fine rings.

Drain the potatoes, allow the steam to evaporate, cut in half and arrange on a buttered baking sheet. Season lightly with salt and pepper, mix the scallion rings with the cheese, and spread over the potatoes. Bake in the preheated oven until golden brown. Remove from the oven and serve immediately. If desired, serve with herb quark on the side.

SERVES 4

8 medium potatoes, waxy variety
3 scallions
scant 1 cup (100 g) grated cheese, e.g. Gouda
salt, pepper

Potato bake with pointed cabbage and bacon slices

Serves 4

generous 1 lb (500 g) pointed cabbage
1 onion
2 tbsp olive oil
1 tsp cumin seeds
1½ tbsp butter
1 tbsp all-purpose flour
1¼ cups (300 ml) milk
½–¾ cup (150–200 g) heavy cream
grated nutmeg
butter for greasing
3 oz (80 g) cooked ham
1¾ lb (800 g) potatoes, waxy variety
¾ cup (80 g) grated cheese, e.g. Emmental
5 slices bacon
salt, pepper

Preheat the oven to 400 °F (200 °C).

Trim the cabbage, pick off 4 nice outer leaves, and blanch briefly in boiling salted water. Drain, rinse briefly in cold water, and pat dry. Cut the remainder of the cabbage in half, separate the leaves from the stalk, and cut into narrow strips.

Peel the onion, chop finely and fry lightly in the olive oil in a hot skillet until transparent. Add the strips of cabbage and 2 tablespoons water, mix in the cumin and simmer gently for 5 to 6 minutes. Season with salt and pepper and remove from the heat. Melt the butter in a pan, stir in the flour, brown lightly, and gradually stir in the milk and the cream. Simmer gently for 4 to 5 minutes until thick and creamy, and season to taste with salt, pepper, and nutmeg. Line a buttered ovenproof dish with the cabbage leaves.

Cut the ham into strips. Peel the potatoes, rinse, and mix with the cabbage and ham. Fill the dish with successive layers of potato mixture, cheese, and sauce, finishing with a layer of cheese. Top with the bacon slices and bake in the preheated oven for about 45 minutes. Remove and serve in portions.

Tip

Pointed cabbage is very delicate and the leaves quickly turn yellow. Wrapped in a damp cloth it will keep for 2 days in the refrigerator.

Dirk Hoberg

Dirk Hoberg is the head chef at the Hotel Riva restaurant on Lake Constance and since 2008, he has been responsible for the wonderfully diverse cuisine of the gourmet Restaurant Ophelia of this 5-star hotel.

On the way to earning his first Michelin star, which he was awarded in 2012, he worked at the starred Restaurant Tristan on Mallorca and the 3-star Restaurant Schwarzwaldstube of the Hotel Traube Tonbach.

Potato gnocchi with melted cherry tomatoes and baby spinach

Serves 4

For the gnocchi

2¼ lb (1 kg) potatoes, floury variety

1½ tbsp (20 g butter)

3 egg yolks

1⅓ cups (200 g) all-purpose flour

For the sauce

7 oz (200 g) cherry tomatoes

1 shallot

olive oil

a little garlic

5½ oz (150 g) baby spinach

1 tbsp butter

Parmesan

salt, pepper

Boil the potatoes in salted water, peel, and evaporate briefly in the oven at 300 °F (150 °C). Press twice through a ricer and then through a fine-mesh sieve, so that no lumps remain.

Melt the butter and add to the potato, then mix in the egg yolk. Gradually work in the sifted flour. Roll out the dough on a work surface dusted with a little potato starch, or flour, cut into rectangles ⅝ x 1½ inches (1.5 x 4 cm) and roll up round a fork. Boil gently in lightly salted water.

To make the sauce, cut the cherry tomatoes in quarters. Peel the shallot, dice small, and brown lightly in olive oil. Add the tomatoes and "melt" over low heat. Season with salt, pepper, and a little garlic, to taste.

Trim the spinach and remove the larger stems. Put a little butter in a skillet and "brown" lightly (beurre noisette). Then add the spinach, season with salt and pepper, toss once, and turn out immediately onto a paper towel. Mix the potato gnocchi with the melted tomatoes, season to taste and serve in a deep plate. Add the spinach and garnish with Parmesan shavings and raw spinach shreds.

"Frittata" of potatoes, spinach, and red onions

For 1 spring-form pan, about 8½ inches (22 cm) diameter
1¼ lb (600 g) potatoes, waxy variety
butter for greasing
7 oz (200 g) baby leaf spinach
2 red onions
4 eggs
1 cup (250 g) heavy cream
grated nutmeg
1 tsp thyme
2 tbsp freshly shaved Parmesan
2 tbsp freshly chopped flat-leaf parsley
salt, pepper

Preheat the oven to 350 °F (180 °C). Boil the potatoes in a pan of salted water for about 25 to 30 minutes, or until tender. Grease a spring-form pan with butter. Peel and slice the potatoes. Wash the spinach, pull off the leaves, clean, and shake dry. Peel the onions and cut in slices. Mix together the eggs and cream and season to taste with salt, pepper, nutmeg, and thyme. Spread one third of the potato slices in the buttered pan and cover with a few spinach leaves. Repeat this process twice more, until the potatoes and spinach have been used up. Pour over the egg and cream mixture, top with the sliced onions, and bake in the preheated oven for about 25 minutes until golden brown. Sprinkle with the Parmesan shavings and parsley before serving.

Frittata with zucchini

Serves 4
14 oz (400 g) potatoes, waxy variety
14 oz (400 g) young zucchini
2 onions
1 garlic clove
olive oil, for cooking
6 eggs
¼ tsp grated nutmeg
4 tbsp grated Parmesan
2 tbsp (30 g) butter
2 tbsp chopped flat-leaf parsley
salt

Boil the potatoes in a pan of salted water for about 25 to 30 minutes, or until tender. Peel the potatoes and cut into small cubes. Wash and cut the zucchini into small cubes. Peel and slice the onions. Peel the garlic and chop small. Brown the zucchini with the onions and garlic in 3 tablespoons olive oil and fry gently with the lid on until they are almost tender. Leave to cool.

Mix the eggs with the nutmeg, Parmesan, and salt to taste. Heat the butter and 2 tablespoons olive oil together in a skillet. Stir the zucchini and diced potato into the egg mixture. Pour the frittata mixture into the skillet and cook over medium heat until the mixture sets, while constantly loosening the frittata from the edges and base of the pan. As soon as the mixture has set, turn the frittata to cook the underside. Sprinkle with chopped parsley and serve lukewarm.

Spinach and potato strudel with sheep's milk cheese

For 1 strudel
For the dough
1¾ cups (250 g) all-purpose flour
½ tsp salt
1 egg yolk
2 tbsp vegetable oil

For the filling
generous 1 lb (500 g) potatoes, waxy variety
¾ lb (350 g) fresh young spinach
2 onions
2 garlic cloves
1½ tbsp (20 g) butter
3 tbsp (30 g) all-purpose flour
1¼ cups (300 ml) milk
1 unwaxed lemon
2 tbsp olive oil
6 tbsp (50 g) pine nuts
7 oz (200 g) sheep's milk cheese
2½ tbsp (40 g) melted butter
salt, white pepper

Mix the flour and salt together and knead to a smooth dough with the egg yolk, oil, and about ½ cup (120 ml) lukewarm water. Form into a ball and leave to rest for 30 minutes under a hot, damp cloth. Wash the potatoes, put in a pan with just enough water to cover, and boil with the lid on for 30 minutes or until tender.

For the filling, peel the cooked potatoes and cut them into ½ inch (1 cm) cubes. Wash the spinach, pull off the leaves, rinse, and wilt in boiling salted water. Then drain, rinse briefly in cold water, press out as much of the liquid as possible and chop. Peel the onions and garlic and chop finely. Melt the butter in a small pan and stir in the flour. Gradually add the milk, stirring vigorously, until the sauce is free of lumps. Wash the lemon in hot water, grate half the rind, and squeeze out the juice. Flavor the sauce with the grated lemon rind, lemon juice, salt, and pepper.

Preheat the oven to 325 °F (170 °C). Heat the olive oil in a skillet and fry the onions and garlic gently until transparent. Toast the pine nuts in a dry skillet until golden brown. Dice the cheese.

Roll out the dough on a large floured dish towel and, using the back of your hands under the dough, pull it out as thin as possible into a rectangle. The dough should be so thin that you can see through it.

Spread the potatoes, spinach, fried onions, pine nuts, and cheese over the dough, leaving the edges free, and pour over the lemon sauce. Fold in the edges and roll up from the long side, using the dish towel. Line a baking sheet with parchment and arrange the roll on it in a horseshoe shape. Brush with the melted butter and bake in the preheated oven for 50 to 60 minutes. Brush occasionally with the butter.

Switch off the oven, leaving the strudel to rest in it for 10 minutes, and then cut carefully in slices.

CIDRE
BOUCHÉ

Sophisticated and Quick: Fried Dishes

Man must eat, everyone knows that, and what he eats influences his entire being.
Eat lenten food and you will be weak-minded; eat fried food and you will feel strength and courage.
FRANZ GRILLPARZER, 19TH-CENTURY VIENNESE DRAMATIST

Good companions: skillets, pans, and potatoes

Fried and perhaps even served in a skillet, fries, tortillas, and potato noodles have something rustic and down-home about them. The smell of frying recalls evenings spent in mountain huts and around camp fires. A large pan of fries in the middle of the table, with a tasty beer and lively conversation, turn even cold winter evenings into cozy memories.

Potato tortilla

Serves 4
1 onion
1½ lb (700 g) potatoes, waxy variety
2 tbsp clarified butter
7 eggs
2 tbsp grated cheese, e.g. Manchego
grated nutmeg
salt, pepper

Preheat the oven to 350 °F (180 °C). Peel the onion and cut into narrow strips. Peel the potatoes, rinse, slice thinly. Heat the clarified butter in an ovenproof pan and brown the potato slices slowly for 10 minutes, turning occasionally. Then add the onion and fry with the potatoes.

Mix the eggs and cheese together and season with salt, pepper, and nutmeg. Pour over the potato mixture, allow to set, and finish by baking in the preheated oven for 10 to 15 minutes.

Irish Boxty

Wash about two thirds of the potatoes and boil for about 30 minutes, or until soft. Drain, rinse in cold water, peel, and press through a ricer. Peel the remaining potatoes, rinse, grate, and squeeze in a kitchen towel to remove as much liquid as possible.
Separate the eggs and mix the yolks with the flour, baking powder, riced and grated potatoes, and milk. Season with salt and pepper. Beat the egg whites to stiff peaks with a pinch of salt and fold in. Melt a little butter in a skillet and add a ladleful of batter. Fry for about 4 minutes over medium heat, turn, and fry for 4 minutes more until golden brown. Served with flakes of butter.

SERVES 4
generous 1 lb (500 g) potatoes, floury variety
2 eggs
generous 1½ cups (225 g) all-purpose flour
1½–2 tsp baking powder
approx. 1¼ cups (300 ml) buttermilk
salt, pepper
⅓ cup (80 g) butter

Potato and cheese fry with spicy apple and onion purée

SERVES 4

FOR THE APPLE AND ONION PURÉE
1 onion
1 tsp mustard seeds
1 tbsp allspice berries
¼ tsp coriander seeds
11 oz (300 g) apples
2 tbsp olive oil
2 tbsp apple vinegar
1 tsp liquid honey
salt

FOR THE POTATO CAKE
generous 1 lb (500 g) potatoes, waxy variety
2½ tbsp (40 g) butter
generous ½ cup (60 g) grated Gruyère cheese
salt, pepper

For the apple and onion purée: peel the onion and chop finely. Crush the spices in a mortar. Peel the apples, cut in quarters, remove the core, and cut the apples in small cubes.
Heat the oil in a pan and gently fry the onion until transparent. Add the spices and fry briefly with the onion. Then add the diced apple, mix in, and add the vinegar. Add about 3½ tablespoons (50 ml) water and flavor with honey, and salt to taste. Simmer over medium heat for 5 to 8 minutes.
Meanwhile, peel the potatoes, rinse, and slice wafer thin. Melt the butter in a hot skillet and arrange some of the potato slices slightly overlapping to form a rosette (about 5 inches/12 cm in diameter), season lightly with salt and pepper, and fry for 3 to 4 minutes until golden brown.
Spread the cheese over the middle of the rosette, leaving a free edge of about ¾ inch (2 cm). Form some more potato slices into another rosette on top and turn the rosette over. Fry for a further 3 to 4 minutes and season with salt and pepper. Arrange on plates and serve with the apple and onion purée.

Tortilla with tomatoes

SERVES 4
1¼ lb (600 g) potatoes, waxy variety
¾ lb (350 g) tomatoes
1 onion
2 garlic cloves
2 tbsp olive oil
4 eggs
scant ½ cup (50 g) grated Manchego cheese
salt, pepper

Boil the potatoes in a pan of salted water for about 20 minutes until tender. Cut the tomatoes into cubes about ½ inch (1 cm) thick. Peel and dice the onion. Peel the garlic and chop finely. Preheat the oven to 400 °F (200 °C). Peel the potatoes and cut into ¾ inch (2 cm) cubes. Fry the onions lightly in 1 tablespoon olive oil until transparent. Add the potatoes to the skillet and fry for 5 minutes. Season to taste with salt and pepper.
Mix the eggs and cheese together in a bowl. Mix the potatoes into the egg and cheese mixture. Heat the remaining 1 tablespoon oil in an ovenproof pan and add the diced tomatoes. Spoon the potato mixture over them, and bake in the preheated oven for about 20 minutes.
Remove the tortilla from the oven and allow to cool for about 10 minutes before serving.

Potato pockets with an apple and onion filling

Serves 4
14 oz (400 g) potatoes, floury variety,
salt

For the compote
11 oz (300 g) ripe apples
3½ tbsp (50 g) sugar
1 cinnamon stick
2 cloves
scant ¼ cup (50 ml) dry white wine

For the dough
1⅓ cups (200 g) all-purpose flour
2 eggs
salt, pepper, grated nutmeg

For the filling
1 onion
5½ oz (150 g) bacon strips

Other
butter and sugar for the baking pan
flour for the work surface
1 egg white
2½ tbsp (40 g) melted butter
6 tbsp (100 g) heavy cream

Wash the potatoes and boil in salted water for 25 to 30 minutes, or until tender. Drain, rinse in cold water, peel, and press through a ricer while still hot. Allow the mash to cool.

Meanwhile peel the apples, cut in quarters, remove the core, and dice small. In a pan, bring to a boil with the sugar, cinnamon stick, and cloves and add the white wine. Simmer over medium heat for about 10 minutes. Remove from the heat, remove the cinnamon and cloves, and leave to cool.

Mix together the flour, eggs, 1 pinch salt, and the cooled potato mash, and with floured hands, work it into a smooth, elastic dough. Season with salt, pepper, and nutmeg. Form into a ball, wrap in plastic wrap, and refrigerate for 30 minutes.

For the filling: peel the onion and chop finely. Cut the bacon strips into small pieces. Render the bacon in a dry pan, brown lightly, add the onion and fry with the bacon for a further 2 minutes. Mix the bacon and onions with the apple compote. Butter the inside of an ovenproof pan and sprinkle with sugar.

Preheat the oven to 350 °F (180 °C). Roll out the potato dough on a well-floured work surface to a thickness of ¼ inch (0.5 cm) and cut out circles of diameter 3 inches (8 cm). Spoon compote onto one half of each circle, brush the edges with egg white, fold the other half over, and press the edges together firmly with the tines of a fork. Put the filled pockets in the prepared pan, brush with a little melted butter, and bake in the preheated oven for 20 to 25 minutes, or until golden yellow. Add the cream 10 minutes before the end of baking time. Remove from the oven and serve with salad or sauerkraut as desired.

Bärner röschti – Bernese rösti

SERVES 4
2¼ lb (1 kg) potatoes, waxy variety
salt, pepper
3 tbsp clarified butter
2 tbsp milk

On the previous day, if possible, wash the potatoes and boil in just enough water to cover in a pan with the lid on for 30 minutes, or until tender.

Peel the potatoes, grate, and season with salt and pepper. Heat the clarified butter in a non-stick skillet, add the potatoes and form into a cake with a spatula. Drizzle with the milk, cover, and fry over very low heat for about 25 minutes, or until crisp. Turn carefully, using the lid or a plate to help you, and fry briefly on the other side over slightly higher heat until crisp. Serve hot.

Wholesome dumpling fry-up

SERVES 4
8 medium-sized dumplings left over from the previous day
1 onion
1 tbsp butter
1½ cups (200 g) diced ham or pancetta
salt, pepper
1 small red bell pepper
2 scallions
3 eggs

If on a Monday morning you have potato dumplings (see p. 160) left over from the Sunday roast, this dumpling fry-up is a perfect way to use them up.

Cut yesterday's potato dumplings into slices about ½ inch (1 cm) thick. Peel the onion and chop finely. Heat the butter in a skillet and fry the diced ham until golden brown. Add the chopped onion, fry with the ham until transparent and season with pepper. Spread this mixture evenly over the base of the skillet. Place the dumpling slices on top and brown on both sides.

Cut the bell pepper into small cubes. Wash the scallions and cut in small rings. Beat the eggs in a bowl. Mix the chopped bell pepper and scallion rings into the beaten eggs and pour over the browned dumpling slices. Cook until set, divide into portions with a spatula, season with salt to taste, and serve.

Potato fry-up with green beans and lemon zest

SERVES 4
9 oz (250 g) green beans
1¾ lb (750 g) potatoes, predominantly waxy variety
1–2 tbsp clarified butter
1 garlic clove
½ bunch scallions
1 small unwaxed lemon
salt, pepper

Wash the beans, trim off the ends and cut into pieces about 1¼ inches (3 cm) long. Blanch in boiling salted water for about 5 minutes, remove, rinse in cold water and leave to drain.

Peel the potatoes, rinse, and cut into ¾ inch (2 cm) cubes. Heat the clarified butter in a large non-stick skillet and fry the potatoes for 12 to 15 minutes, turning occasionally.

Meanwhile, peel the garlic clove, chop finely, and fry with the potatoes. Trim the scallions, rinse and cut in fine rings. Wash the lemon in hot water, rub dry, and zest or finely grate the rind. Add the beans to the potatoes and fry for about 5 minutes, until the potatoes and beans are tender. Season the fry-up with salt and pepper and flavor with the lemon zest. Sprinkle with the scallion rings and serve.

Tyrolean Gröstl

Peel the onion and chop finely. Wash the potatoes and boil in a pan of salted water for 25 to 30 minutes, or until tender.

Peel and slice the potatoes. Cut the meat into strips. Melt the clarified butter and fry the potatoes for about 5 minutes until golden brown. Mix the onion in with the meat and fry for a further 4 to 5 minutes. Sprinkle with the parsley, season to taste with salt, pepper, and cumin to taste, and serve.

Serves 4

1 onion
2¼ lb (1 kg) potatoes, waxy variety
14 oz (400 g) cold roast pork
2 tbsp clarified butter
1 tbsp freshly chopped parsley
ground cumin
salt, pepper

Gnocchi, Dumplings, and Potato Noodles

After a good dinner one can forgive anybody.
OSCAR WILDE, 19TH-CENTURY IRISH POET AND DRAMATIST

Potato side dishes

Potatoes are often underrated as a side dish, merely there to fill people up, when in fact they round off a main dish perfectly. Imagine Thanksgiving turkey without mash, burgers without French fries or a soda without potato chips. Where would the Italians be without gnocchi or the British without fish and chips? Potatoes soak up the sauce and enhance it with their own flavor. Of course they are filling as well, though not only as supporting actors but also when playing the lead.

Florentine potato roll

SERVES 4
2¼ lb (1 kg) potatoes, floury variety
1¼ lb (600 g) fresh leaf spinach
2 shallots
1 garlic clove
1 tbsp olive oil
1 pinch grated nutmeg
2 egg yolks
1 egg
7 tbsp (50 g) grated Parmesan
1¾ cups (250 g) cornstarch
generous ¾ cup (200 ml) hot milk
salt, pepper

Wash the potatoes and boil in a pan with just enough water to cover, with the lid on, for 30 minutes, or until tender. Trim and wash the spinach and leave to drain. Peel the shallots and garlic, chop finely, and fry lightly in a pan in hot olive oil until soft. Add the spinach to the pan, wilt, then press very firmly to remove as much liquid as possible, chop coarsely, and leave to cool. Mix the spinach, the egg yolks, and the Parmesan, and season with salt, pepper, and nutmeg. Peel the potatoes, press through a ricer while hot, sift over the cornstarch. Beat the egg and the milk together, season with salt, pepper, and nutmeg, mix in thoroughly. On a damp kitchen towel, roll out the potato dough to a rectangle about 14 x 10 inches (35 x 25 cm). Spread the spinach evenly over the dough and form into a roll with the help of the kitchen towel. Wrap the towel around the roll and tie at both ends. In a roasting pan or sufficiently large saucepan, bring plenty of salted water to a boil and simmer the spinach roll over low heat for 30 minutes. Unwrap the roll, slice, and serve.

VARIATION
Leeks cut in thin rings and lightly fried can be used instead of spinach.

TIP
If any of the potato roll is left over, it can be sliced and fried, or topped with Parmesan and baked.

Aligot—French potato and cheese purée

SERVES 4
2¼ lb (1 kg) potatoes, floury variety
3 garlic cloves
10 tbsp (150 g) crème fraîche
7 tbsp (100 g) salted butter
2½ cups (300 g) grated Comté cheese
salt, pepper

This substantial purée was a traditional meal for shepherds. Although it is very filling, it is absolutely delicious.

Peel the potatoes and boil in just enough salted water to cover, with the lid on, for 30 minutes, or until tender. Drain, evaporate a little, and mash. Peel the garlic, crush in a garlic press and add to the potatoes. Slowly mix in the crème fraîche, butter, and grated cheese, until the purée forms "strings" as you lift it. Season with pepper to taste and serve immediately.

Potato cake with broccoli and mozzarella

SERVES 4
1¾ lb (800 g) potatoes, waxy variety
1 onion
11 oz (300 g) broccoli
1 ball mozzarella
6 eggs
4 tbsp olive oil
grated nutmeg
salt, pepper

Peel the potatoes and grate coarsely. Peel the onion, chop finely, and mix with the grated potato. Cut the broccoli into florets, wash, blanch in boiling salted water, rinse in ice cold water, and drain thoroughly. Cut the mozzarella in slices.

Preheat the oven to 375 °F (190 °C). Beat the eggs into the potatoes and season the mixture with salt, pepper, and nutmeg. Fold in the broccoli. Brush the inside of a gratin dish or a cast iron skillet with half the olive oil and spoon in the mixture. Spread the mozzarella over it and drizzle with the remaining olive oil. Bake on the middle shelf of the preheated oven for 30 minutes. Serve straight from the oven.

Classic gnocchi

SERVES 4
(AS A MAIN COURSE)
2¼ lb (1 kg potatoes), floury variety
1¾ cups (250 g) all-purpose flour
1 egg yolk
1 pinch grated nutmeg
flour for dusting
scant 1 cup (100 g) grated Parmesan
salt

Wash the potatoes and boil in a pan with just enough water to cover, with the lid on, for about 25 minutes, or until tender. Drain, evaporate thoroughly, and peel.

While still hot, press the potatoes through a ricer into a bowl. Add the egg yolk, flour, salt to taste, and nutmeg, and knead to an elastic dough. Set aside the gnocchi dough to rest for 10 minutes.

Roll the dough out in "ropes" about ¾ inch (2 cm) in diameter, dust with a little flour, cut into pieces about ¾ inch (2 cm) long and press with a fork, so that ridges can be seen. Bring plenty of salted water to a boil and simmer the gnocchi over low heat until tender. When they rise to the surface, scoop out with a slotted spoon, serve on warmed plates, and sprinkle with Parmesan.

VARIATION

Gnocchi can also be served with tomato sauce or sage butter, or topped with mushrooms and baked.

TIP

Gnocchi are very suitable for freezing.

Potato dumplings

SERVES 8
4½ lb (2 kg) potatoes, floury variety
2 tbsp white wine vinegar
generous ¾ cup (200 ml) milk
3 tbsp cornstarch
1 stale bread roll
3½ tbsp (50 g) clarified butter
salt

These are eaten in Bavaria and Franconia, and also in Thuringia where they are prepared in a slightly different way.

Peel a generous 1 lb (500 g) of the potatoes, cut in quarters and boil in plenty of salted water for 20 minutes, or until soft. Meanwhile, peel the remaining potatoes and grate finely in a food processor or on a vegetable grater. Mix the grated potato with the white wine vinegar. Then squeeze a portion at a time in a kitchen cloth to extract as much liquid as possible, collecting it in a bowl. Leave the potato water to stand for a little, until the potato starch has sunk to the bottom. Pour off the water and add the potato starch to a bowl, along with the raw potatoes.

Drain the cooked potatoes and mash, or press through a ricer. Bring the milk to a boil and add to the mash. Add the cornstarch and a large pinch of salt to the raw potatoes and work into an elastic dough. Cut the bread roll into small cubes, fry in the clarified butter until crisp, and leave to cool.

In a large pan, bring plenty of salted water to a boil. Wet your hands and form 12–16 dumplings, pressing two or three cubes of fried bread into the middle of each. Put the dumplings in the boiling water and simmer over low heat for about 25 minutes or until tender. Scoop out with a slotted spoon and drain thoroughly.

Bavarian "half-silky" dumplings

SERVES 4
generous 2¼ lb (1 kg) potatoes, floury variety
4 slices white bread
3½ tbsp (50 g) clarified butter
generous ¾ cup (200 ml) milk
1⅓ cups (200 g) potato flour
1 pinch grated nutmeg
salt

Wash the potatoes and boil with just enough water to cover in a pan with the lid on for 20–25 minutes, or until tender. Meanwhile, cut the bread into small cubes, fry in the clarified butter until crisp, and set aside.

Peel the potatoes and press through a ricer while still hot. Briefly bring the milk to a boil, add to the potato flour with the salt and nutmeg, knead to an elastic dough, and leave to rest for 15 minutes.

Bring plenty of salted water to a boil. Flour your hands and form the dough into 8 to 10 dumplings, with a few cubes of fried bread in the middle of each.

Put the dumplings in the gently boiling salted water and simmer for about 20 minutes until tender. Scoop out with a slotted spoon and serve.

Potato-harvest bonfire

In the fall, the nights get longer and the air is cooler. At the end of a long harvest season whole families stand around the fire and enjoy its pleasant warmth as it spreads throughout their bodies.

In earlier times there was a very practical reason for the end-of-harvest fire. The farmers burned the remains of the potato plants in order to completely destroy any contagious germs. The fire was a very effective weapon against blight and other potato diseases.

Once it was necessary, now it is simply fun and gives us an opportunity to celebrate the end of summer, throw a few potatoes into the fire with family and friends, and eat bread cooked on sticks. The burning flames have exercised a deep fascination on people for many thousands of years, offering a feeling of security, even though winter is not far away. If there is something delicious to eat as well, it makes the fall evening perfect.

Of course you may not live in a place where you can simply light a bonfire in your garden to burn the garden waste, but if you can keep a safe distance away from your house and your neighbors you might be able to install a brazier or make a fire with a stack of small bits of wood. Lay a little circle of stones around your fire so that it cannot spread out of control.

Stockbrot — Bread on a stick

Serves 6

3½ cups (500 g) all-purpose flour
1 package active dried yeast
1 tsp salt
1 cup (250 ml) water
1 tbsp olive oil

In a bowl, mix together the flour, dried yeast, and salt, make a well in it and add the water and olive oil. Working inward from the outside, knead all the ingredients to a smooth dough, cover, and leave to rise in a warm place for 1 hour.

Then knead the dough again and on a floured work surface form into 6 evenly-sized balls. Roll these balls out into long thin strips and wind each one round the end of a stick. Hold the "Stockbrot" over the fire, turning continuously to prevent it from burning.

Tip

Hazel twigs are very good for Stockbrot, as they are long, straight, and not too heavy. The sticks can also be used several times. Anyone who does not want to wind the dough directly on to the stick, can wrap a little aluminum foil round the end of the stick first.

Potatoes à la croque monsieur

Serves 4
4 large potatoes (each about 11 oz/300 g), floury variety
2 tsp cumin seeds
4 fairly thick slices of Comté or Appenzeller cheese (about 7 oz/200 g)
4 slices cooked ham
3½ tbsp (50 g) butter
salt, pepper

Wash the potatoes, put in a pan with just enough water to cover, add the cumin, and boil for 35 to 40 minutes, or until tender. Allow to cool a little and peel. Cut the potatoes in half lengthwise and cut the underside of each half so they lie flat and do not roll about.

Preheat the oven to 400 °F (200 °C). Season the upper surfaces of the potatoes with salt and pepper. Cut the slices of ham in half and cut the cheese to fit the potatoes. Between each pair of potato halves place half a slice of ham, then a slice of cheese, and lastly the second half of the ham.

Tie the potatoes together with kitchen string and arrange in a greased gratin dish. Top with flakes of butter and bake in the preheated oven for 15 to 20 minutes, until the cheese begins to melt. Remove the potatoes from the oven and remove the string.

Franconian potato noodles

Wash the potatoes, put in a pan with just enough water to cover, with the lid on, and boil for 30 minutes, or until tender. Peel and allow to cool completely or cook the day before.

Press the cold potatoes through a ricer, or grate on a vegetable grater. Add ⅔ cup of flour and eggs, season with salt, pepper, and nutmeg and knead to a dough, gradually adding more flour (up to ⅓ cup), if necessary, to achieve a firm dough. Roll pieces of the dough between the palms of your hands to form thick noodles about 4 inches (10 cm) long. Preheat the oven to 350 °F (180 °C) and brush a gratin dish with the oil. In a large skillet, fry the noodles on all sides in hot clarified butter for about 8 minutes, then transfer to the gratin dish and bake on the middle shelf of the oven for a further 20 minutes, or until ready.

Serves 4

2¼ lb (1 kg) potatoes, floury variety

⅔ – 1 cup (100 – 150 g) all-purpose flour, depending on the consistency of the dough

1 large egg or 2 small eggs

1 tbsp oil

clarified butter for baking

grated nutmeg

salt, pepper

Baden Bubenspitzle with sauerkraut

Serves 4–6
2¼ lb (1 kg) potatoes, floury variety
1 large onion
7–8 strips (100 g) bacon
1 tbsp oil
1 jar or can sauerkraut (1¼ lb/580 g)
1 cup (250 ml) meat stock
1 bay leaf
2 juniper berries, crushed
⅔–1 cup (100–150 g) all-purpose flour (amount depends on the consistency of the dough)
1 large or 2 small eggs
grated nutmeg
clarified butter, for frying
salt, pepper

During the 30-Years War, in the first half of the 17th century, the soldiers made noodles from their allotted ration of flour plus water. They only developed into the much finer Bubenspitzle many years later with the addition of potato.

Wash the potatoes, put in a pan with just enough water to cover, and boil with the lid on for 30 minutes, or until tender. Peel and allow to cool completely or cook the day before. For the sauerkraut, peel the onion, chop finely, and cut the bacon into small pieces. Fry the onion and bacon lightly in the oil, then add the sauerkraut, meat stock, bay leaf, and juniper berries, cover, and fry over low heat for about 45 minutes. Season with salt and pepper to taste.
Meanwhile, press the cold potatoes through a ricer. Add ⅔ cup of flour and eggs, season with salt, pepper, and nutmeg and knead to a dough, gradually adding more flour (up to ⅓ cup), if necessary, to achieve a firm dough. Roll pieces of the dough between the palms of your hands to form noodles about 1 inch (2.5 cm) thick. In a large pan, bring plenty of salted water to a boil and simmer the noodles in it for about 3 minutes until tender. Remove from the pan with a slotted spoon and drain well. Heat the clarified butter in a large skillet and brown the noodles on all sides. Serve with the sauerkraut.

Tip
Serve a dry white wine with these noodles. With Bubenspitzle as a basis, there is nothing to stand in the way of an extensive wine-tasting session in congenial company.

Skubenken – Czech potato noodles with onions

SERVES 4
2¼ lb (1 kg) potatoes, floury variety
6 tbsp butter
generous 1⅔ cups (200 g) all-purpose flour
2 eggs
2 large onions
1 pinch grated nutmeg
salt, pepper

Peel the potatoes, cut in quarters, put in a pan, just cover with salted water, and boil with the lid on for about 15 minutes, or until tender. Drain and press through a ricer into a bowl while still hot. Allow to cool a little, then mix together with 2 tablespoons of the butter, the flour, and the eggs. Season well with salt, pepper, and nutmeg, and knead into an elastic dough.

In a large pan, bring plenty of salted water to a boil. With floured hands form the potato dough into noodles about 3 inches (8 cm) long and 1 inch (2.5 cm) thick. Simmer the potato noodles in the salted water over low heat, without the lid on, for about 15 minutes, or until tender.

Meanwhile, peel the onions and chop finely. Heat the remaining butter in a skillet and fry the onions, turning continuously. Scoop the potato noodles out of the salted water with a slotted spoon and drain very thoroughly on paper towels. Arrange on a warmed serving dish and spread the fried onions over them.

VARIATION

The potato dough can also be formed into little flat cakes and fried in hot clarified butter until golden brown. Fresh, finely chopped herbs or chopped ham can also be mixed into the potato dough.

Potato pizza with cherry tomatoes and mozzarella

SERVES 4
1½ lb (750 g) potatoes, floury variety
2 onions, 2 garlic cloves
7 oz (250 g) mozzarella
generous 1 lb (500 g) cherry tomatoes
1⅔ cups (200 g) all-purpose flour
2 tsp baking powder
4 eggs
3 tbsp olive oil
1 tsp each of thyme and oregano (less if using dried herbs)
salt, pepper
fat for greasing

Peel the potatoes, boil in salted water for about 20 minutes, or until tender, drain, and allow to cool a little. Peel the onions and garlic and chop finely. Cut the mozzarella in small cubes. Preheat the oven to 400 °F (200 °C). Wash the cherry tomatoes and cut in halves. Drain the potatoes and mash in a fairly large bowl. Mix the flour, baking powder, eggs, and salt to taste, into the mashed potato. On a baking sheet lined with parchment, roll out the dough to about ¾ inch (2 cm) thick, and drizzle with the olive oil. Top with the onions, garlic, cherry tomatoes, mozzarella, and herbs and bake on the middle shelf of the preheated oven for about 30 minutes.

Cakes and Breads

Why sing of the rose, aristocrat? Sing of the democratic potato that feeds the people!
HEINRICH HEINE, 19TH-CENTURY GERMAN POET, JOURNALIST, ESSAYIST, AND LITERARY CRITIC

Sweet and satisfying

When you think of potatoes, the first thing that comes to mind is probably not cakes and sweet dishes. However, anyone who has ever sampled a potato cake will have fallen for its delicate juicy flavor. In plum dumplings or potato waffles, potato bread, or potato soufflé, potatoes are full of surprises. Some also offer a genuine, healthy alternative for anyone who is allergic to wheat.

Potato bread

MAKES 2 LOAVES
9 oz (250 g) potatoes, floury variety
3 cups (450 g) bread flour + extra for the work surface
2 tsp sugar
1 package dry active yeast
generous ¾ cup (200 ml) warm milk
3½ tbsp (50 g) butter, at room temperature
salt

Peel the potatoes and put in a pan, just cover with water, add salt to taste, and boil for with the lid on, for about 25 minutes, or until tender. Measure out ⅔ cup (100 g) of the flour and tip into a bowl. Add the yeast to the bowl with the sugar and the warm milk and mix everything together. Cover and leave to rise in a warm place for 15 minutes.

Line a baking sheet with parchment. Press the hot potatoes through a ricer into a bowl and leave to cool. Then add them to the bowl containing the yeast mixture, mix together, and slowly knead in the remaining flour. Turn the dough out onto a floured work surface, knead well again with your hands, and divide in two. Form into two loaves of equal size, transfer to the baking sheet, and cover with a kitchen towel. Leave to rise for a further 30 minutes.

Preheat the oven to 425 °F (220 °C). Bake the potato bread on the middle shelf of the preheated oven for about 40 minutes, remove from the oven, and leave to cool on a wire rack.

TIP
Potato bread also freezes very well.

Potato and onion layer cake

SERVES 4–6
1¾ lb (800 g) potatoes, floury variety
generous 1 lb (500 g) onions
4 tbsp olive oil
2 sprigs thyme
1 cup (250 ml) vegetable stock
salt, pepper

Preheat the oven to 400 °F (200 °C). Peel the potatoes and onions and slice thinly. Brush the inside of a 10-inch (26-cm) diameter cake pan with 2 tablespoons of the olive oil. Arrange alternate layers of potato and onion slices in the pan, with the slices slightly overlapping. Season with salt and pepper.

Rinse the thyme under running water, strip off the leaves, and scatter over the vegetables. Drizzle with the remaining olive oil and pour over the vegetable stock.

Cover with aluminum foil and bake on the middle shelf of the preheated oven for 45 to 50 minutes. Remove the foil 15 minutes before the end. Can be served fresh from the oven or cold.

Potato kugelhopf with almonds

Peel the potatoes and put in a pan. Just cover with water, add salt to taste, and boil with the lid on for about 25 minutes, or until soft. Drain, evaporate, and allow to cool. Then press through a ricer into a bowl.

Preheat the oven to 350 °F (180 °C). Put the butter, sugar, and vanilla in a bowl and beat to a foamy batter with an electric hand whisk or mixer, adding the eggs one at a time. Add the riced potatoes. Then sift in the flour, baking powder, and cocoa. Add the ground almonds, and raisins and mix well.

Grease a kugelhopf cake pan and sprinkle with breadcrumbs. Spoon in the cake mixture and bake on the middle shelf of the preheated oven for 50 minutes. Remove from the oven, tip out of the cake pan, and leave on a wire rack to cool completely. Lastly, dust with confectioner's sugar.

Serves 12

14 oz (400 g) potatoes, floury variety
1¾ cups (250 g) butter, + extra for greasing
1 cup + 2 tbsp (250 g) sugar
1 tsp vanilla extract
5 eggs
2⅓ cups (350 g) all-purpose flour
5 tsp baking powder
5 tbsp cocoa
⅔ cup (100 g) ground almonds
¾ cup (100 g) raisins
salt
breadcrumbs for the pan
confectioner's sugar for dusting

Potato and apricot bread with saffron

MAKES 2 LOAVES
9 oz (250 g) potatoes, floury variety
¼ tsp (1.3 g) powdered saffron, or to taste
4 cups (500 g) spelt flour + extra for work surface
1½ packages active dry yeast
1 cup (125 g) dried apricots
2 tbsp honey
⅓ cup (80 g) butter, at room temperature
2 egg yolks
1 egg white
salt
1 tsp poppy seeds for sprinkling

TIP
The bread is ready when it sounds hollow if you tap the underside.

Peel the potatoes and put in a pan. Just cover with water, add a little salt, and boil with the lid on, for about 25 minutes, or until soft. Drain, but reserve the cooking water. Press the hot potatoes through a ricer into a bowl. Mix the saffron with 1 cup (250 ml) of the reserved cooking water and add to the bowl.

Mix the flour with a pinch of salt and the dried yeast. Dice the apricots small. Add the potatoes, honey, butter, egg yolks and diced apricots to the flour mixture. Using the dough hook of a hand mixer, work everything together for about 5 minutes to an elastic dough. Cover the dough and leave to rise for about 40 minutes at room temperature. Line a baking sheet with parchment.

Preheat the oven to 400 °F (200 °C). Knead the dough again, this time by hand, on a floured work surface. Divide in two, form into two round loaves, and place on the baking sheet. Cover, and leave to rise for a further 30 minutes.

Whisk the egg white, brush the loaves with it, and sprinkle evenly with poppy seeds. Bake the loaves on the middle shelf of the preheated oven for about 40 minutes until golden brown, remove from the oven and leave to cool on a wire rack.

Apple and potato bread with cumin

MAKES 1 LOAF
7 oz (200 g) potatoes, floury variety
3½ cups (500 g) bread flour + extra for work surface
2 ripe eating apples
1¼ cups (300 ml) milk
1 package active dry yeast
2 tbsp cumin seeds
salt
butter for the pan

The previous day, if possible, wash the potatoes and boil in salted water for 25 to 30 minutes, or until soft.

Press the potatoes through a ricer and mix them with the flour. Wash the apples, peel, cut in quarters, remove the cores, grate finely and mix with the potato flour.

Warm the milk and stir in the yeast. Leave in a warm place to ferment then pour into the flour. Using the dough hook of an electric hand mixer, work into a smooth dough, working ⅔ of the cumin seeds into the dough. Cover the dough and leave to rise in a warm place for 45 minutes, until it doubles in volume.

Preheat the oven to 350 °F (180 °C). Knead the dough again on a floured work surface and form into a loaf. Sprinkle the loaf with the remaining cumin seeds, transfer to a greased baking pan and bake in the preheated oven for 50 to 60 minutes until golden brown. Remove from the oven and allow to cool before serving.

Bohemian plum dumplings

SERVES 4 – 6

generous 1 lb (500 g) potatoes, floury variety
20 plums
20 sugar cubes
generous 1 cup (150 g) flour
1 cup + 2 tbsp (250 g) butter
2 egg yolks, salt

FOR THE CRUMB

7 tbsp (100 g butter)
1 cup (50 g) breadcrumbs
2 tbsp brown sugar
cinnamon

VARIATION

Apricots can be used instead of plums.

Wash the potatoes and boil in a pan with the lid on, in just enough water to cover, for about 25 minutes, or until soft. Peel the hot potatoes, press through a ricer into a bowl, and allow to cool.

Meanwhile, wash the plums, cut open lengthwise, remove the pits, and replace with sugar cubes. Add the flour, 2 tablespoons (30 g) butter, the egg yolks, and a pinch of salt to the cooled potatoes and knead together to give an elastic dough, adding a little more flour if necessary.

Divide the dough into 20 pieces. Press each piece flat and wrap it round a plum, pressing the "seam" together firmly. Bring plenty of salted water to a boil, add the dumplings and simmer for 8 to 10 minutes in lightly bubbling water. They are ready when they float to the surface.

Meanwhile, melt the butter in a skillet, add the breadcrumbs, sugar, and cinnamon to taste, and fry until golden brown. Remove the dumplings from the pan with a slotted spoon, drain, and roll in the crumbs. Lastly pour over any remaining melted butter.

Potato and coconut purée

Peel the potatoes, cut in quarters, and boil in just enough water to cover, for about 20 minutes or until soft. Drain and press through a ricer or a fine sieve into a casserole. Mix in the butter, coconut milk, and heavy cream. Slit the vanilla bean open lengthwise, scrape out the seeds and mix them into the purée along with the sugar and coconut flakes. Serve the potato purée in individual dishes, sprinkled with coconut flakes.

Serves 4–6

11 oz (300 g) potatoes, floury variety
3½ tbsp (50 g) soft butter
¼ cup (50 g) heavy cream
3½ tbsp (50 ml) coconut milk
1 vanilla bean
3½ tbsp (50 g) sugar
½ cup (30 g) coconut flakes + plus some for decoration

Almond and potato noodles with apple compote

Peel the apples, cut in quarters, remove the cores and chop the apple segments coarsely. Put them in a pan with the white wine, honey, and cinnamon stick and cook gently over low heat for 30 minutes. Remove from the heat, remove the cinnamon stick, and allow the apples to cool.

Peel the potatoes, cut in quarters, put in a pan with just enough salted water to cover, and boil for about 15 minutes, or until soft. Drain and press through a ricer into a bowl while still hot and leave to cool a little. Then mix the potato to a dough with 2 tablespoons of the butter, the flour, ground almonds, and eggs.

In a large pan bring plenty of salted water to a boil. With floured hands, form the potato dough into noodles about 1 inch (2.5 cm) thick and about 3 inches (8 cm) long. Drop the potato noodles into the boiling salted water and simmer over low heat for about 15 minutes without a lid.

Meanwhile, mix the sugar with the cinnamon. Melt the remaining butter and use a little to toast the chopped almonds. Remove the potato noodles from the salted water with a slotted spoon and drain thoroughly.

Toss briefly in the remaining melted butter, then arrange on 4 individual plates, sprinkle with the cinnamon sugar and chopped almonds, and serve with the apple compote.

Serves 4

1¾ lb (800 g) apples
7 tbsp (100 ml) dry white wine, e.g. Riesling
2 tbsp honey
1 cinnamon stick
2¼ lb (1 kg) potatoes, floury variety
4 tbsp butter
1 cup (150 g) flour (if possible, coarse-grained wheat flour) + extra for handling
4 tbsp ground almonds
2 eggs, beaten
2 tbsp sugar
2 tsp ground cinnamon
chopped almonds
salt

Thomas Kellermann

Thomas Kellermann is the highly successful chef at the Burg Wernberg hotel in the Bavarian Oberpfalz. He was awarded a second Michelin star in 2011. He favors a classic cuisine with the emphasis on vegetables.

Potato cocktail with an apple and sorrel sorbet

Serves about 15

There are quite a few steps involved in preparing this potato cocktail, but it is worth the time and effort when you want to serve something different to a fairly large group. One step leads to another, and the last one produces a wonderful sorbet.

Sorrel yogurt

1 bunch sorrel
7 tbsp (100 ml) milk
8 tbsp Greek yogurt
salt, white pepper

First mix the sorrel with salt and pepper to taste, stir in the milk and pass through a sieve.
Mix the Greek yogurt with about 3 tablespoons of the sorrel milk and season again to taste with salt and freshly ground white pepper. Pour the finished yogurt into chilled cocktail or dessert glasses.

Potato cream

2 leaves gelatin
¾ lb (350 g) boiled, sieved potatoes, floury variety
1 cup (250 g) Greek yogurt
10 tbsp (150 g) whipping cream
salt, white pepper
1 pinch grated nutmeg

Soak the gelatin in water. Mix the potatoes with the yogurt and season to taste with salt, pepper, and nutmeg. Dissolve the softened gelatin in a little warm cream and add to the potato yogurt. Whip the remaining cream and fold into the potato yogurt. Now spread half the potato cream on top of the sorrel yogurt in the serving glasses. Mix the remaining potato cream with the remaining sorrel milk and add this as the next layer.

Shallot sauce

4 cups (1 liter) poultry stock
8 shallots
5 tbsp white balsamic vinegar
2 tbsp hot mustard
generous ¾ cup (200 ml) oil
salt, white pepper, sugar

Reduce the poultry stock to one quarter. Peel the shallots, dice finely, and blanch briefly. Mix with the vinegar and mustard and whisk in the oil and the reduced stock. Season to taste with salt, pepper, and sugar. Pour the sauce gently over the potato and sorrel cream until it is completely covered.

Sorrel foam

Using a hand blender, whisk all the ingredients to a foam and put about 2 tablespoons in each of the filled cocktail glasses.

6 tbsp (100 g) sour cream
3½ tbsp (50 ml) mineral water
salt, white pepper
lime juice, a little sugar

Apple and sorrel sorbet

Cut the unpeeled apples in quarters, remove the cores, and cut in chunks. Heat gently with the sugar and water. Then purée in a blender, leave to cool, and then purée again, together with the lime juice and sorrel. Pass through a sieve and freeze in an ice cream maker.

Scoop out peaks of sorbet with a teaspoon and put one on each potato cocktail.

4½ oz (125 g) apples, e.g. Granny Smith
⅓ cup (75 g) sugar
1 cup (250 ml) water
juice of 2 limes
about 10 sorrel leaves

Potato chips

Squeeze the juice out of the potatoes. Warm the juice, stirring continuously, until it thickens. Season to taste with salt and white pepper.

Preheat the oven to 350 °F (180 °C). Spread thinly over a baking mat and bake for about 8 minutes. (Check the chips are not over-browning.) Remove from the oven and leave to cool. Then cut into long triangles, lay on a sheet of parchment, and sprinkle with a little smoked paprika powder. To finish, bake for about 3 minutes at 350 °F (180 °C), but check.

Garnish the cocktail glasses with the potato chips.

10 potatoes, floury variety
salt, white pepper
smoked paprika powder

Potato waffles

Makes 10 – 12 waffles
9 oz (250 g) potatoes, floury variety
4 eggs, separated
¾ cup + 2 tbsp (120 g) flour
4 tbsp (60 g) soft butter
6 tbsp (100 ml) heavy cream
2 tsp grated zest from rind of an unwaxed lemon
4½ tbsp (60 g) sugar
salt
oil for the waffle iron

Boil the potatoes just covered in water for 30 minutes, or until soft, peel, press through a ricer, and leave to cool. Mix the egg yolks, flour, butter, cream, and grated lemon zest into the riced potatoes. Beat the egg whites in peaks with the sugar, a pinch of salt, and fold into the potato mixture.

Preheat the waffle iron to medium and brush both cooking surfaces thinly with oil. Spoon 2 – 3 tablespoons of mixture on to the lower surface and bake the waffles for 3 – 5 minutes until golden yellow. Serve freshly made and, for example, with vanilla ice cream and seasonal berries.

Potato soufflé

Wash the potatoes and boil in just enough water to cover for 25 minutes, or until soft. Peel, press through a ricer, and leave to cool. Mix the potato purée with the heavy cream and the orange liqueur. Preheat the oven to 350 °F (180 °C). Stir the yolks evenly into the potato mixture. Beat the egg whites, cornstarch, and confectioner's sugar to very stiff peaks and fold evenly into the mixture.
Grease a 2½ quart (1.5 liter) soufflé dish and fill with the mixture, leaving an edge about 1¼ inches (3 cm) wide. Bake on the bottom shelf of the preheated oven for 30 to 40 minutes. Do not open the oven during cooking, as this will cause the soufflé to collapse. Remove from the oven, dust with confectioner's sugar, and serve immediately.

Serves 4
11 oz (300 g) potatoes, floury variety
generous ½ cup (150 ml) heavy cream
3 tbsp orange liqueur, e.g. Cointreau
4 eggs, separated
1 tsp edible cornstarch
4 tbsp confectioner's sugar
butter for greasing
confectioner's sugar for dusting

Potato and quark cake with apple

For 1 spring-form pan 10 inches (26 cm) diameter
9 oz (250 g) potatoes, floury variety
1 apple
3½ tbsp (50 ml) Calvados
juice of ½ lemon
3 eggs, separated
⅔ cup (150 g) sugar
1 cup (250 g) quark, 20% fat
⅓ cup (50 g) all-purpose flour
5 tsp baking powder
1 tbsp cornstarch
salt
fat for greasing
confectioner's sugar for dusting

Boil the potatoes in just enough water to cover for 30 minutes, or until soft. Peel, press through a ricer, and leave to cool.

Peel the apple, cut in quarters, grate coarsely, and mix with the lemon juice and Calvados. Beat the yolks to a foam with the sugar and mix into the riced potatoes along with the quark, flour, baking powder, and cornstarch.

Preheat the oven to 350 °F (180 °C) and grease the spring-form pan. Beat the egg whites with a pinch of salt to very stiff peaks and fold evenly into the potato mixture. Spoon the batter into the pan and bake on the middle shelf of the preheated oven for about 50 minutes. Allow to cool, then dust with confectioner's sugar.

Shredded potato pancake

Serves 4
1¼ lb (600 g) potatoes, floury variety
generous ¾ cup (200 ml) milk
4 eggs, separated
5 tbsp sugar
salt
1 tbsp edible cornstarch
3½ tbsp (50 g) clarified butter
salt
confectioner's sugar for dusting

Wash the potatoes, put in a pan, cover with water, and boil with the lid for 30 minutes, or until soft. Then peel and mash. Bring the milk to a boil and pour over. Beat the whites to stiff peaks with a pinch of salt.

Preheat the oven to 375 °F (190 °C). Mix the egg yolks, sugar, and a pinch of salt into the potato mixture, then fold in the egg whites evenly.

Heat the clarified butter in a large ovenproof pan and spoon in the potato mixture. Bake on the middle shelf of the preheated oven for about 20 minutes. Remove from the oven, tear into bite-size pieces using two forks, dust with confectioner's sugar, and serve.

Tip

Serve with home-made plum or cherry compote. You can also add a dash of Kirschwasser or other cherry-based alcohol to the dough.

Sourdough potato bread

Makes 1 loaf
7 oz (200 g) potatoes, waxy variety
2⅓ cups (350 g) wheat flour
1 cup (150 g) rye flour
3 tsp (10 g) fresh yeast
1¼ cups (300 ml) lukewarm water
2 egg whites
5½ oz (150 g) store-bought sourdough starter
1 tsp sea salt

Boil the potatoes in a little water with the lid on for about 30 minutes, or until soft. Then peel and press through a ricer. Mix the wheat flour and rye flour together in a bowl and make a well in the middle. Crumble the yeast and add to the bowl, pour over 7 tablespoons (100 ml) of the lukewarm water and mix with the yeast. Cover the dough and leave to rise for 20 minutes. Beat the egg whites to stiff peaks. Add the beaten egg white, riced potatoes, sourdough starter and sea salt to the pre-dough, along with the remaining water and work into an elastic dough.

Grease a baking sheet or line with parchment. Knead the dough again firmly by hand for 10 minutes, form into a long loaf and place on the baking sheet. Cover with a damp kitchen towel and leave to rise for 1 hour. Preheat the oven to 475 °F (240 °C). Spray the oven with a little water (this will help to form a good crust). Bake the bread on the middle shelf for about 40 minutes. Remove from the oven, leave to cool on a wire tray, and eat while as fresh as possible.

Potato bread with ham and olives

Add the yeast to the lukewarm water. Mix the flour and salt in a bowl, make a well in the middle, pour in the yeast and the oil and knead to a smooth dough that comes away from the sides of the bowl. Turn out on to a floured work surface, knead thoroughly for about 10 minutes, return to the bowl, cover and leave to rise in a warm place for about 1 hour.

Preheat the oven to 400 °F (200 °C). Peel the potatoes, rinse, and grate. Knead into the dough along with the cheese and ham, and roll out into two flat loaves ¾ inch (1.5 cm) thick. Place on a baking sheet lined with parchment and leave to rest for a further 15 minutes.

Slice the olives and spread over the loaves along with the rosemary. Drizzle with olive oil and bake in the preheated oven for 25 to 30 minutes. Remove from the oven, allow to cool a little, cut in pieces, and serve lukewarm.

MAKES 2 FLAT LOAVES

1 package active dry yeast
1 cup (250 ml) lukewarm water
3½ cups (500 g) flour + extra for dusting
1 tsp salt
2 – 3 tbsp olive oil
9 oz (250 g) potatoes, waxy variety
generous ½ cup (60 g) grated Parmesan
3½ oz (100 g) Parma ham, chopped
3 oz (80 g) black olives, pitted
a few sprigs rosemary
olive oil for drizzling

Index of recipes

Index of names and terms

Useful addresses

USA

Whole Foods Market: www.wholefoodsmarket.com
Southwind Farms: www.southwindpotatoes.com
Larsen Farms: www.larsenfarms.com
United States Potato Board: www.uspotatoes.com

UK

Potato Council: www.potato.org.uk
Whole Foods Market: www.wholefoodsmarket.com

Photo credits

Bayerischer Bauernverband: pp. 38, 128
Fotolia: pp. 30 both, 31 bottom, 79 all, 81 middle, 81 bottom, 163
Alexander and Eva Fuchs: p. 40 all
Dirk Hoberg: p. 132
iStockphoto: pp. 8, 31 top, 39, 41
The Munich Potato Museum, Stiftung Otto Eckart: pp. 12, 13, 14, 15 both, 16, 17
Thomas Kellermann: p. 180
Christine Paxmann: p. 81 top
Dr. Margit Roth: p. 19 all
Shutterstock: cover 1
Sissy Sonnleitner: p. 122

Stockfood: cover 4 all, pp. 4 right, 5 both, 7, 11 all, 20, 23, 24, 26, 27 both, 28 both, 29 all, 32, 35 all except bottom right, 36 both, 42 both, 43 right, 44 all, 45 all, 46, 49, 50, 51, 53, 55, 56, 57, 59, 63, 65, 67, 68, 71, 73, 77, 83, 85, 89, 91, 92, 93, 94, 95, 96, 99, 101 all, 103, 105, 106, 109 all, 111, 113, 115, 116, 117, 121, 123, 125, 127, 129, 131, 133, 135, 137, 138, 141 all, 142, 143, 145, 147, 149, 151, 151, 152, 155 all, 157, 159, 161, 164, 165, 167, 168 both, 170, 173, 175, 177, 178, 181, 182, 183, 185, 186, 187

WMF Deutschland: pp. 35 bottom right, 43 left

Abbreviations and quantities

1 oz = 1 ounce = 28 grams
1 lb = 1 pound = 16 ounces
1 cup = 8 ounces = 16 ounces
1 cup = 8 fluid ounces = 250 milliliters (liquids)
2 cups = 1 pint (liquids)
8 pints = 4 quarts = 1 gallon (liquids)
1g = 1 gram = 1/1000 kilogram
1kg = 1 kilogram = 1000 grams = 2 1/4 lb
1 l = 1 liter = 1000 milliliters (ml) = approx 34 fluid ounces
125 milliliters (ml) = approx. 8 tablespoons
1 tbsp = 1 level tablespoon = 15–20g (see below) = 15 milliliters (liquids)
1 tsp = 1 level teaspoon = 3–5g (see below) = 5ml (liquids)

Disclaimer

The information and recipes printed in this book are provided to the best of our knowledge and belief and from our own experience. However neither the author nor the publisher shall accept liability for any damage whatsoever which may arise directly or indirectly from the use of this book.

It is advisable not to serve dishes that contain raw eggs to very young children, pregnant women, elderly people, or to anyone weakened by serious illness. If in any doubt, consult your doctor. Be sure that all the eggs you use are as fresh as possible.

Original Title: *Gute Kartoffeln. Die große Liebe zur kleinen Knolle*
ISBN 978-3-86362-009-7

Editor: Dr. Margit Roth
Project management: Marion Koschkar
Layout and design: Christine Paxmann text · konzept · grafik, Munich

Translation from German: Rae Walter in association with First Edition Translations Ltd, Cambridge, UK
Editing: Lin Thomas in association with First Edition Translations Ltd, Cambridge, UK
Typesetting: The Write Idea in association with First Edition Translations Ltd, Cambridge, UK

Overall responsibility for production: h.f.ullmann publishing GmbH, Potsdam, Germany

Printed in India, 2015

ISBN 978-3-8480-0807-0

10 9 8 7 6 5 4 3 2 1
X IX VIII VII VI V IV III II I

www.ullmann-publishing.com
newsletter@ullmann-publishing.com
facebook.com/ullmann.social